Ian McKellen

Best wishes

08

Karate

for

Children

Volume 1 - Basics

By
Shihan John van Weenen
MBE OMT 8th Dan

Other books by the same author:

'The Beginner's Guide to Shōtōkan Karate'
Paperback, ISBN 0-951-7660-4-X £14.95 in UK
In Funakoshi's Footsteps: Autobiography 530 pages
Hardback, ISBN 0-9517660-5-8 £14.95 in UK
In Funakoshi's Footsteps: Autobiography 530 pages
Paperback, ISBN 0-9517660-9-0 £9.95 in UK
Advanced Shōtōkan Karate Kata
Paperback, ISBN 0-9517660-1-5 £12.95 in UK
Task Force Albania - An Odyssey
Paperback, ISBN 0-951-7660-8-2 £9.95 in UK
Task Force Albania - The Kosovo Connection.
Paperback, ISBN 0-951-7660-3-1 £9.95 in UK

Karate for Children Vol. 2 - Kata and **Karate for Children Vol. 3 - Kumite**
Both Hardback, full colour, A4 format, now in production

* * *

Acknowledgements:
Martin Stevenson, Olney Health & Fitness Centre, Olney, Bucks.
Tim Brown - Layout Artwork, Emma Blenkinsop - Illustrations, Robin Tucker -
Photography, TASK students: Hannah Walsh, Jessica Whalley, Naomi Meakin, Danielle
Reddington, Jessica Mondon, Kai Kanno, Rosanna Haskell, Georgia Barnaby, Jai Singh,
Haydn van Weenen, Richard Danenberg, Tariq Mani-Saada, Junior Advisor, Sam Harding -
Proof Reading, Philip Smith 4th Dan

Karate for Children Volume 1, Basics. ISBN 978-0-9555180-0-3   Hardback, Price £14.95

Printed by: Butler and Tanner Ltd, Tel: 01373 451500 Website: www.butlerandtanner.com

Distributed by:
Vine House Distribution Ltd. Waldenbury, North Common, Chailey, East Sussex BN8
4DR. England. Tel: 01825 723398. Fax: 01825 765649. E-mail: sales@vinehouseuk.co.uk.
Website: www.vinehouseuk.co.uk
Blitz Corporation Ltd., Unit 10, The I.O. Centre, Duke of Wellington Avenue, Royal
Arsenal, London. SE18 6SR Tel: 0208 3032276. Fax: 0208 3195799
E-mail: elida@blitzsport.com Website: www.blitzsport.com
Playwell Martial Arts, Playwell House, 30-31, Sheraton Business Centre, Wadsworth Road,
Perivale, Middlesex. UB6 7JB Tel: 020 8810 9449 Fax: 020 8810 9779
E-mail: accounts@playwell.co.uk Website: www.playwell.co.uk

Master Gichin Funakoshi

1869 - 1957

The Father of Modern-Day Karate-dō

"Make benevolence your lifelong duty. This surely is an important mission. It is a lifelong effort, truly a long journey."

This book is dedicated to all Children,
but especially those who are
practising Karate-dō,
for they will become the teachers of tomorrow.

Preface

'**I** remember well writing the preface for the first edition of 'The Beginner's Guide to *Shōtōkan Karate*' in November 1983. At that time, very few children were practising the art, consequently, it was written in general with adults in mind.

It concentrated purely on the three basic aspects of *Karate* training; *Kihon, Kata* and *Kumite* Much to my surprise, it became a best seller and was used by students and instructors alike.

Today, things are entirely different. Adults are no longer attracted to *Karate* as they once were and four out of every five beginners are children whose ages range between five and ten years. The need for an elementary children's book was overwhelming.

After much research I decided to produce '*Karate* for Children', breaking it down into three separate volumes. Each would have an A4 hardback format, be in full colour, and show children performing the necessary techniques.

Into each volume, I have endeavored to introduce a wealth of essential information for all young people starting out in *Karate*, but with an overriding theme of 'fun' as a priority.

Indeed, producing these books has been an enlightening experience for me, and an enormous privilege to work with so many talented youngsters, many of whom are destined to become tomorrow's teachers.'

John van Weenen
June 2007

About the Author

J ohn van Weenen was born in 1941 and spent his early years in Enfield, Middlesex. At school he proved to be an exceptional swimmer, representing England in 1956. By the early 1960's, he had developed a deep interest in the Martial Arts but was frustrated by the lack of available information on them.

In 1964, he emigrated to Australia and soon after arriving in Adelaide, joined a *Karate* club, run by the late Moss Hollis, a 3rd Dan to whom John will always remain indebted. Almost three years later, after training four or five nights a week, he was awarded his Black Belt.

John returned to England in late 1966, where he established the first *Karate* club in North London. People came from all over the capital to his *dōjō* in Enfield, to learn of this new and fascinating art.

The Club affiliated to the '*Karate* Union of Great Britain' and *Hirokazu Kanazawa* 5th Dan was the Chief Instructor. In July 1967, *Kanazawa Sensei* relinquished his position and returned to Japan. More than anything, John wanted to go too. The Japanese Embassy in Grosvenor Square told him it was impossible. Undeterred, he set out with two fellow students, across Europe and Asia and finally arrived at Yokohama.

The training sessions at the JKA Headquarters in Tokyo were at worst 'severe', and at best, 'inhospitable'. In retrospect, they were of enormous benefit - providing one survived!

Receiving his 3rd Dan Diploma from Master Kanazawa

The following year he returned to the U.K. after having hitch-hiked 3,000 miles across North America and so began his life as a professional *Karate* teacher. In the 40 years that have followed, John has taught *Karate-dō* to tens of thousands of people from all walks of life and many of today's National Chief Instructors, began their *Karate* training in one of his *dōjō*.

Whilst adhering strictly to the teachings of *Kanazawa Sensei*, whom John himself regards as the 'greatest teacher of modern times', he was unknowingly being drawn more and more towards the doctrines and philosophy of *Gichin Funakoshi*.

By 1991, fate had taken a hand and John found himself leading the largest convoy of humanitarian aid to leave the UK since World War II. The route lay through war-torn Yugoslavia to the tiny country of Albania, who's citizens were dying of starvation under communist oppression.

Harnessing his 27 years of practising *Karate-dō* and with the assistance of a loyal team of *Karateka*, the aid finally got through and without any form of physical violence whatsoever.

Two years later on a lonely mountain road he met Albania's most famous daughter - 'Mother Teresa'. *'Make benevolence your lifelong duty. This surely is an important mission. It is a lifelong effort, truly a long journey.'* They were the words of *Funakoshi*, written 50 years earlier but they could just as well have been hers - their philosophy was indistinguishable.

These days, much of John's time is spent as the Honoury Consul for Albania here in Gt. Britain, working with his son Haydn in the family Estate Agents, and teaching and writing about *Karate-dō*.

Foreword

I have known John van Weenen for more years than I care to remember, yet there are times, quite inexplicably, when I feel I don't know him at all. When a helping hand was needed in war-torn Albania and Kosovo, primarily for the orphaned children, I knew John would be there - and he was.

Conversely, in a time when very little karate reference material was available, I knew John would provide it, which he did with his best selling books: 'The Beginner's Guide to Shōtōkan Karate' and 'Advanced Shōtōkan Karate Kata'.

However, with a growing child based participation audience, the possibility of John writing a book dedicated to children never ever occurred to me. With hindsight it should have.

His four decades of teaching and much respected position within the global fraternity of senior karateka have made him the obvious choice for such a work.

Having been privileged to read a preview script, I can only say, 'I underestimated his exceptional ability to communicate to younger people.'

John's understanding of the child's view or mindset is something to be revered. He has captured completely that much needed guidance and presented it in what can only be described as the 'the perfect format.'

I would urge any child or serious practitioner of Karate to put their orders in now for volumes 2 (Kata) and 3 (Kumite) as they are sure to sell out fast. I would also like to openly congratulate John and thank him for producing such a superb book, providing a much needed reference work for the growing army of young karateka around the world.

Although it's not a word I usually subscribe to, if asked to suggest one word to describe; 'Karate for Children', it would be *awesome*.

I can't wait to see volumes 2 and 3 and neither can my children, Paige and Pierce. 'C'mon John, let's see Volume 2 - now!'

Paul S. Clifton

Publisher - Combat Magazine.
Traditional Karate Magazine.
TaeKwonDo & Korean Martial Arts Magazine.
Fighters & Kickboxing News Magazine.

Contents

2

4

Finding the right *Karate club* for you, and the right *Sensei!*

So - you're learning *Karate* either in school time, at an after-school class, or alternatively you may be training at a local club.

Practising at school leaves you no choice in who teaches you, whereas with a local club, you have greater freedom.

Start by asking yourself some questions:

1) Is your teacher good?
2) Do you like him?
3) Is he strict sometimes?
4) Does he have fun?
5) Are the lessons enjoyable?
6) Does he teach by showing you?

If your answer to all these questions is 'yes', you've got the right teacher.

Should the other students be covered in bandages, this is not a good sign, so choose your club carefully!

Explanation of these points:

Your teacher is the single most important aspect of learning *Karate*. He needs to be a good teacher but his experience doesn't always guarantee this.

If you like him, you'll do your best, but if you fear him, there'll be no trust on your part. He needs to be firm and strict at times to instil discipline, but not an ogre. Although serious at times, the lesson needs to be fun and enjoyable.

A good teacher will teach by example. He will not only tell you what to do, he will also show you, which enables you to copy correctly.

Postscript (of special interest to parents)

If your child is learning *Karate* in school time or at an after-school club, it is no guarantee the teacher is proficient. The responsibility lies with the head teacher to make sure the *Karate* instructor is a recognised authority on his subject, and is approved by the country's governing body. He should have been Criminal Records Bureau (CRB) checked and in possession of a current instructors liability insurance policy.

'Sensei – where did Karate come from?'

Alex Breeds from Olney in Buckinghamshire. had asked the question during a weekly after-school class. 'That's an interesting question' I replied, and gestured for the class to come around and sit down.

'A long time ago, in the far off land of Tibet, were a group of monks who practised the Buddhist Faith. During the course of their work, as they travelled from one part of the country to another, spreading the teachings of Buddha, they often came under attack from robbers. This happened frequently on lonely mountain paths that connected outlying villages.

As their religion forbade them from carrying weapons of any kind, the monks developed a method of self-defence. During the 6th and 7th centuries, they became very effective fighters, and later when they journeyed eastwards to spread the teachings of Buddha to Mongolia, they took their method of

Monks travelling along lonely mountain paths

self-defence with them.

From there, in the following years, it spread into China where it fused with many other fighting forms before eventually reaching the island of Okinawa in the East China Sea. It is thought shipwrecked sailors introduced a fighting art to Okinawa in the 14th Century.

The Okinawans embraced it and combined it with the local fighting systems to become known as *'Tode'*, pronounced, (toe-day).

In 1915, The Father of modern-day *Karate, Gichin Funakoshi*, successfully introduced it into Japan where in 1955, The Japan *Karate* Association was formed. Ten years later, *Karate* arrived here in Great Britain, and many other European countries too.'

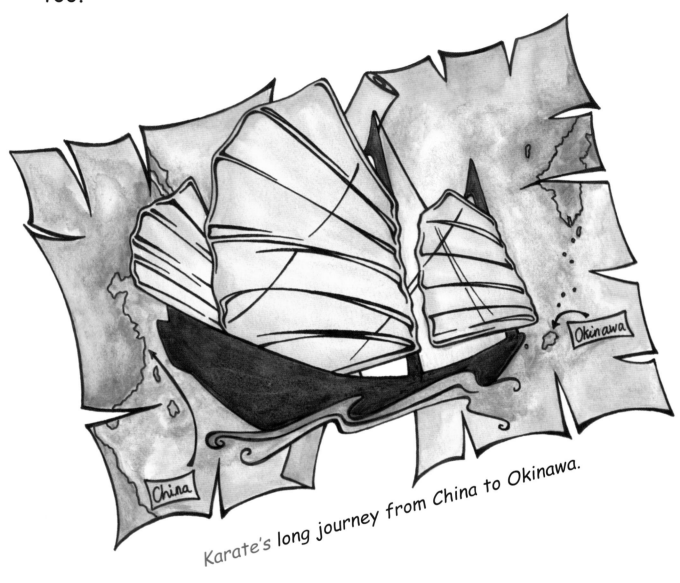

Karate's long journey from China to Okinawa.

'Mr Miyagi, tell me about good manners - er please'

'Certainly Daniel San
As you know, the belt system in *Karate* is very important. Wearing a coloured belt means you have reached a certain level, taken an examination and passed.

Good manners Daniel San are caring for others. A similar word for manners is etiquette. Being correct both in and out of the *dōjō* is very important. The higher you go in grade, the better your etiquette should become.'

With that, Mr. *Miyagi* drew his chair closer to Daniel's. 'Think of it like this Daniel San.

You must always be on time for training, arriving a few minutes early with a clean *Karate-gi*. As you know, we never eat, drink or smoke in the *dōjō*, and we make sure our finger and toe nails are cut, so as not to cause injury to anyone.

We wear only our *Karate-gi* - no rings, necklaces or jewellery of any kind, with one exception, girls may wear a T shirt under their practice suit. Never, Daniel San, walk through the streets, or arrive by car wearing your practice suit. Change into it at the *dōjō*, (not in the *dōjō*), and after training, take a shower before folding your *Karate-gi* correctly.

Always think of the *dōjō* as a special place - it may be a school hall, gymnasium or multi-purpose room, nevertheless, it's your *dōjō* and deserves respect.

Bow on entering or leaving the *dōjō* and before joining or leaving a class. Bow to your instructor first, then to fellow students when seeing them for the first time or departing, and remember Daniel San, a lower grade should always bow to a higher grade first.

In my country, a student will enter the *dōjō* and bow to all the instructors individually - *highest grade first.*

Now I hear you say Daniel San, how do you know who is the highest grade - they are all wearing black belts?

You must make it your business to find out!

A bow too, after an instructor has corrected your technique is a must.

Always be polite and courteous to other *Karate-ka*

at the *dōjō* as well as outside it. Carry this on to all you meet everywhere.

Finally Daniel San, learn the *Dōjō-Kun* and live it every day of your life. If you do this, you will become a good *Sensei* yourself and I will be very proud of you - but Daniel San - *Miyagi* very proud now.'

Sensei – A Special Teacher

Once-upon-a-time, in the far off country of Okinawa, lived an old man. His wife had died and his sons had grown up and left the family home.

Every morning very early, he would wake up, wash, and clean his teeth before putting on his long flowing black gown.

After a breakfast of fruit, raw cabbage and green tea, he would walk for an hour or so amongst the many pine trees that surrounded his house. They were tall and stretched almost to the sky. He loved the fresh smell of pine needles and the rustling of the upper branches in the wind.

After his walk, it was to his small *dōjō* behind his house that he would return to begin his daily training. For two-hours he would go through the motions of punching, kicking, striking and blocking. Although he was old, his movements were still performed with power and despite his advancing years, he had lost little of the speed that was a hallmark of his youth.

Soon, students began arriving at the *dōjō*, and

entered quietly, all with the deepest of bows to their *Sensei*. To them, he was the greatest teacher in the land - not only a teacher of *Karate*, but also a teacher of life, and as such, they loved him.

In 1957 he died, at the age of eighty-eight.

Countless students both far and wide, but especially those in Japan and Okinawa were saddened deeply. Strangely, amongst all his personal students who mourned his passing, there existed an

unexplainable, yet underlying feeling of great happiness. You see - they had known *Sensei*, and had been privileged to be part of his life and share his wisdom.

Now it was their turn to become *Sensei*, teach all they had learned - and more! In time, so much more!'

Bowing –
why do it?
We're British!

In the East (China, Japan), people greet each other with a bow, and in doing so, are showing respect for one another. Here in Great Britain, as in other western countries, we shake hands.

The bow then, is more than a handshake. It is a greeting, a salutation, and a special way for human beings to communicate with each other. In practising what is essentially an Okinawan/Japanese martial art, it is only proper we retain the bow and exercise the respect and tradition that it implies.

It must be performed correctly, as the shape of the person's body who is bowing, indicates how he or she feels towards the other person.

When bowing, the heels should be together, feet turned out at 45 degrees and the body bent at the waist. The back should be kept straight, head down, but with the eyes looking forward towards the other persons feet. It is disrespectful to look into someone's eyes whilst bowing. It says 'I trust you - but not that much!'

Always remain in the downward position for about one second, before returning to the upright position once again.

A word like no other

If an adult was asking the meaning of the word *'oss'*, I'd probably say something like: It's a relatively unique way of expressing *Karate* spirit whilst at the same time providing a minimalist method of communication between *Karate-ka*.

However, as you the reader are almost certainly under ten years of age, may I put it like this:

Oss (spoken as in - boss) is a special word for the *Karate* student. It can mean almost anything. For example: Hello, goodbye, see you later, how are you, good to see you, I understand, thank you, yes, no and many more.

It helps the young student gain *Karate* spirit, and at the same time, encourages a response (gets him or her to speak). Not long complicated passages, but a short, sharp *'oss'* forcing air up from the stomach *(hara)* whilst thinking of the words he would normally use.

After several years of saying *'oss'*, the person you are saying it to will understand what you mean, without actually saying it in English.

Wow! How does that work? Here's how to find out. Open up your dictionary and look up the word *'telepathy.'*

It's quite amazing, but it works. Just be patient and in time you will discover you have a *sixth-sense*, which may turn out to be your best friend. On the other hand always remember 'the journeying may be better than the arrival'.

Now you really will have to ask your Mum or Dad what that means!'

The Dōjō – It's your special place

A dōjō is a place where you train in *Karate*. It may be a hall, gymnasium, room or indeed any space indoors or outdoors where you practise. With so many places available, hundreds if not thousands, why should each space be special?

The answer lies not in the hall or room, but what you think about it *in your head*.

A good *Karate* student thinks of a dōjō, any dōjō, as a special place where he or she is very lucky indeed to be able to go and practise.

A student must care for the dōjō, look after it, and always treat it with respect. That is why we always bow upon entering and leaving.

We never abuse or damage it. The dōjō is purely a place we come to practise and improve our *Karate* techniques, and we would never dream of eating, drinking or smoking within it.

To those outside *Karate*, it is just a hall, but to you the *Karate-ka*, it is your special place. A way place. Your *Karate* home.

A busy dōjō

How to tie
your belt

There is no one set way of tying a belt. Different martial arts have their own method. *Judō* for example has the belt tied at the waist, whilst *Karate-ka* tie theirs lower down over their hips.

The following is a traditional Japanese way of tying a belt for those who practise *Karate*.

Although tied around the hips, the belt when tied, should be lower in the front than the back. The knot should be central and positioned three inches below the navel at the body's physical and spiritual centre of gravity. The tightness of the belt should be such, as to allow a slight pressure from the knot on the stomach (this helps the student remember where his stomach is)!

So - hold the belt in both hands (pic.1). Bring the middle of the belt to your navel (pic.2) and pass both ends around your back and bring them to the front (pic.3). Both ends are of equal length at this point.

Twist the belt to the right so the left hand end is about four inches longer than the right (pic.4). Take the left-hand (longer) end over the right-hand end and pass it under the whole belt (pic.5). The longer end is now on the right.

Now take the end on the right (still the longest) over the one on the left (pic.6) up through the loop, and pull both ends into a knot (pic.7). Both ends should be of equal length.

Black belts often have their name on the right-hand side end and their association or style on the left-hand end. Both are usually in Japanese characters, the association being written in *Kanji* (taken from China), whilst the name of the owner is written in *Katakana* or *Hiragana* (for ease of translation).

The Japanese people have three alphabets to contend with compared to our one in English. Aren't we lucky?

Breathing

Breathing *(Kokyu)* is of the utmost importance in the practice of *Karate-dō*. When learning basics, breath is inhaled through the nose during the first part of the technique, and exhaled via the mouth at the end of the technique. Exhaling as the movement is concluded aids muscle contraction (tensing) and assists *Kime* (focus).

Many breathing practices exist and depend on the speed and number of movements being performed. For example, in a punching combination, the out-breath should be devided between the number of punches. Basic breathing exercises employed in *Karate* often have a 'Tai Chi' background and therefore have a distinct Chinese influence.

Breathing from the stomach and diaphram is encouraged from the outset of *Karate* training, as opposed to breathing from the chest. Using the whole of one's lungs rather than just a portion of them is of great benefit, and develops the chest through the expansion and contraction of the connective tissue. Without a doubt, and most importantly, it also aids longevity (long-life).

How to fold your Karate-gi

In *Karate-dō*, there is a correct way of doing everything. Even a menial task such as folding a *Karate-gi* should be undertaken with precision and sincerity.

After each training session, your *Karate-gi* should be washed and ironed, before being folded and placed in your *Karate* bag. On no account should it be worn on your way to the *dōjō*.

Your practice suit is important, as too is the way you treat it, and your attitude towards it. It should always be folded a certain way.

In children it encourages a routine, a pattern of behaviour that has to be

A mother carefully irons her son's Karate-gi

adhered to. To put it simply, it encourages a discipline and through it, self discipline.

A Parent's Guide

The overwhelming case for children to learn *Karate*

The following is offered purely to highlight the benefits of *Karate* training for children. It may be of assistance if your child is thinking of taking up the art and you need more information as to what it entails.

The views stated are my personal ones, that together with my senior instructors, we endeavour to instil. Other instructors may have different ideas as to what constitutes acceptable behaviour, and obviously I can't speak for them.

Ultimately, you the parent must be the judge as to where you place your child to learn *Karate*, but please remember - the most convenient place for you, may not be the best place for them.

Even to the staunch traditionalist, *Karate* training is forever changing and this is perfectly natural as our knowledge of the human body increases.

To the *Karate* teacher, children are not miniature adults. Their physiology differs enormously as too do their levels and types of fitness. Children's bones are not fully formed and adult exercises can cause permanent damage. Bearing these points in mind, the case for children's involvement in *Karate* cannot be ignored.

Thirty years ago, the average *Karate* class consisted of about 2% children and 98% adults. Today, 80% of students are children under the age of 14. The reason for this massive increase stems largely from, 'just how beneficial *Karate* training can be for young people'. Most traditional martial arts have the same effect but I speak as a *Karate* teacher only and one who has a limited knowledge of other disciplines.

Children are taught from the outset that *Karate* is primarily defensive and not offensive. They are taught never to use their fighting skills outside the *dōjō* (training hall), except in cases of extreme provocation and then only to defend. Apart from the physical aspects, everything else practised in the *dōjō* must be practised in the course of their life.

Etiquette:

A boy or girl during the first few weeks of their training learns and practises basic etiquette. They learn to be polite and respect their fellow students, instructor and parents. Soon, they become aware that good manners consist of having consideration for other people.

Discipline:

Young people react to discipline very well considering how little many seem to get of it on the domestic front. Many parents often absolve themselves of all responsibility in this department, transferring the load to the already overburdened school-teacher. Once a child has been disciplined for a short period, he then develops self-discipline and behaves correctly, of his own free-will.

His concentration is enhanced as he focuses his mind on the job in hand, whether it may be learning a sequence of complicated moves or passing an exam at school. Many parents notice a marked improvement in their child's powers of concentration once *Karate* training has commenced. Ironically however, not all are prepared to acknowledge publicly that the *Karate* instructor may have been instrumental in achieving this.

In my opinion, children should not be made to think of themselves as failures. 'These adults of tomorrow' should be encouraged in everything they do. How many times do you hear a parent shouting at a child, telling him 'you're stupid', 'you're terrible', 'you should be ashamed of yourself'. Say them enough and the child will think of himself and grow up, stupid, terrible and ashamed. On the other hand - praise, compliment and encourage him and you will have a child who is confident, well balanced and a pleasure to be with.

Self Confidence:

Karate wins hands down on this score every time, but is it any wonder many children lack confidence in themselves? Just look at many parents - they do. From birth, children learn by mimicking the parent's actions. Can you blame a child for being tense and nervous after observing his parents desperate attempts to 'make ends meet' and cope with the enormous pressures of 21st century living.

Traditional *Karate* training helps prepare a child for life. I find it enormously encouraging when a mother or father who brings a child to lessons, does not just dump them, and head straight for the nearest pub, but instead, comes into the *dōjō*, sits down and takes an interest in what their child is learning. Children love to perform, especially to the people closest to them and they are far more clever than we give them credit for. How often are 'little cries for help' disregarded. Rejection, to a child from questions like 'come and play with me', or read, or walk or do anything, can be very hurtful, especially when the child has heard it one hundred times before. Answers like: 'I haven't got time', 'later', or 'I'm busy', do nothing to inspire confidence.

When children come to my *Karate* lessons, I tell them that for the next hour I'm going to treat them like adults. When the lesson is over, they will walk out of the *dōjō* and their parents and the world will treat them again like children. The response I get is nothing short of amazing. Just watching 7-year-olds standing next to grown men and women, learning together is quite something. The children know more is expected from them and with a little encouragement from the teacher, they rise to the occasion.

Fitness:

As a method of keeping fit, *Karate* is almost without equal. Many adults find it difficult to stay in good shape, whereas children find it a lot easier, consequently, they enjoy it more. A healthy body promotes a healthy mind.

Self-defence:

Growing up in the early 'fifties, apart from scraps that all boys get into, I cannot remember seeing much street violence or hearing of muggings, although I'm sure it must have gone on.

Fifty years on, things do appear to have changed somewhat. Today, muggings take place in every town in the country. No longer are young people the only victims; now elderly folk are considered 'fair game'. Consequently, I feel a basic knowledge of self-defence is essential for young people.

Training for life:

The psychological theme running through each lesson epitomises the triumph of good over evil. It encourages a gentlemanly code of conduct and the necessity to maintain standards. Discipline, etiquette and respect for one's elders all have their place in *Budō*, the code of the military man. To relate, communicate and co-exist peaceably with one's fellow man is an ideal worth striving for.

Success at school:

Through constant repetition and self-analysis of physical techniques, relative perfection is ultimately acquired. Once this learning technique has become a habit, the principle will automatically be applied to most things by the sub-conscious. Indeed, many parents and school teachers have remarked how their child's powers of concentration have improved since starting *Karate* training. Co-ordination obviously becomes much better as too does the child's awareness factor. The latter without doubt, plays a key role throughout a person's life.

Hygiene

and a Karateka's way of thinking

Traditional *Karate* has always been concerned with all aspects of personal hygiene, especially in the *dōjō*.

A few simple rules need to be observed. In the case of children, they encourage cleanliness, common sense and a code of conduct that will 'stick', remaining with them always. In other words, it is about forming good habits in the *dōjō*, that will be transferred to the home and school.

In the *dōjō*

A student should not enter the *dōjō* unless his *Karate-gi* is clean, his finger and toe nails are cut and he has attended to his personal comforts (visited the toilet prior to training).

No food or drink should be brought into the *dōjō*, or consumed on the premises. Smoking, it goes without saying is to be avoided.

You need only a clean *Karate-gi* and a clean person inside it.

In the home and at school

What the student learns in the *dōjō* concerning hygiene will hopefully continue at home and school. Parents will notice a marked improvement in how their child cares for himself, which may have a knock-on effect for them.

Even at school, teachers and peers (your class mates) alike will be aware of a change in attitude towards cleanliness and hygiene.

Determined to be the cleanest student in the dōjō

How to stop yourself becoming Master or Miss Angry

It's easy! Just close your eyes and allow them to remain closed now and breath *in* through your nose and *out* through your mouth slowly. As you do so, count backwards from 10-1.

For example: Take a deep breath in through your nose and as you breathe out through your mouth slowly, think '10'. Now do the same again and think '9', and so on.

As you reach '1', all traces of anger will have disappeared completely and you will feel calm and relaxed.

As a result, the hurtful things you might have said in anger, you will not say, and you will gain nothing but respect from others.

What is more, it shows how you are in control of

yourself and not at the mercy of someone bent on aggravating you.

Try it. It works every time.'

How to get your next belt

Do you really want to know the answer to this question? If the answer is yes - then read on. If no - then turn over.

Just what does a belt *(obi)* in *Karate* mean?

Yes, you're right, it means you have reached a certain standard, a higher level than before. The different colours make it easy for everyone to know how good you are.

Putting on a new coloured belt shows you have worked hard, sat an examination, passed, and moved on to your next level of training and learning.

But how do you actually get it?

Well I'm afraid it isn't easy. If it were it would have no value - so try this.

Look at the syllabus for your next grade in your favourite *Karate* book. Learn the techniques from your *Sensei* in class and then devote your time to practising them.

Remember - your weekly *Karate* class is the place for learning and being taught new techniques. Your real training should take place away from your club, by yourself, perhaps at home.

Many students fail to realise this and consequently

often remain a poor standard. Your *Sensei* can show you what to do and how to do it. The rest is up to you - *you* have to do it yourself!

That's the best advice I can give you. Practice really does make perfect. Now imagine yourself wearing your next belt and - **go for it!**'

A young Karate student receiving his first belt

Sensei never stops talking about basics. Why?

'What are basics and what makes them so important? Well - think of it like this: The alphabet as you know has twenty-six letters and they are at the heart of the English Language. Without them, there would be no words, no sentences, no paragraphs, no stories, no books and so on.

Now, think of *Karate* basic techniques as the alphabet. Unfortunately, there are not just twenty-six basics - there are literally hundreds.

Once the basics have been mastered (if they ever can be), we can use them in two very distinct areas, namely *Kata* and *Kumite*.

Kata are made up of a collection of basic techniques (which we will go into in much greater detail in Volume II). With over fifty *Kata* still in existence today, assuming an average of thirty moves or basic techniques in each, we are looking at a figure of around one thousand five hundred basic techniques! Wow!

Kumite. The seven separate types of *Kumite* (sparring) that lead to free-sparring *(Jiyū-Kumite)* will be covered in Volume III, and involves hundreds of basic techniques. Now I hope you can see just how important basics are, without them there would be no *Kata* or *Kumite,* as with the alphabet - without it, there would be no English language.

So the next time you hear *Sensei* talking about basics, you'll understand their importance and know why - won't you?'

Are exercises really necessary?

'YES!'

Says 5 year old Tariq

Light Trunk Twisting

Head Slowly Forward and Back

Head Slowly Twisting

Head Slowly Shoulder to Shoulder

Head Slowly Turning in
Half Circles

Arms Circling Forward
and Back

Trunk Bending in
Different Directions

Five Floor Stretching
Excersises

Leg Raising
(Forward)

Leg Raising
(Sideways)

Stretching Inner
Thighs

Right: Pushing The
Back Hip Forward

Below: Stretching for
Side Splits

Stances

As this book is intended primarily for beginners up to black belt *(Shodan)*, the following six stances are initially essential. Later other stances can be introduced, however, a thorough knowledge of these six is vital, as most future *Karate* techniques will utilize them.

Hachiji-Dachi

Natural Open-Leg-Stance
The Natural Open-Leg-Stance is assumed after bowing and on the command of *'yoi'*. The feet are hip-width apart. The right foot moves.

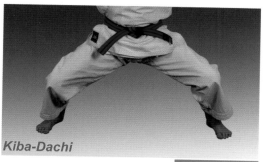

Kiba-Dachi

Straddle-Leg-Stance
Very effective when used in conjunction with side-snap or thrust-kicks. Body weight is spread evenly between both legs and the feet are twice shoulder width apart. Feet should be turned in slightly and knees pushed out - hips pushed down.

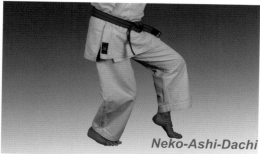

Neko-Ashi-Dachi

Cat-Stance
An artistic yet effective stance mainly used when blocking. With 90% of the body weight over the back leg, this stance is ideal for kicking with the front leg. The heel of the front foot remains off the floor.

Zenkutsu-Dachi

Front-Stance
A strong stance used for blocking and attacking, having 70% of the body weight over the front leg. Feet approximately 3 feet to 4 feet apart and hip-width wide.

Kōkutsu-Dachi

Back-Stance
Used mainly for blocking frontal attacks, having 70% of the body weight over the back leg. The front foot is directly in line with the heel of the back foot and they are 3 feet to 4 feet apart.

Fudo-Dachi

Rooted-Stance
A very strong stance midway between *Zenkutsu* and *Kiba-Dachi*. The body weight is slightly more forward than back. Both feet are at a 45° angle and are twice shoulder width apart, they are also hip-width wide.

Punching

A punch is a way of using the hand to hit or strike someone. Before you can punch, you have to make a fist. This is done by curling the fingers and thumb up to make a clenched fist.

We use the front or Fore-fist *(Seiken)* to hit with. Upon contact, the punching fist must be kept tight.

Punch in Japanese is '*Zuki*'. Just say 'Zoo-key'.

Straight-Punch
Choku-Zuki

1 2 3 4

A Straight-punch is *Karate's* most basic punch, and is usually practised in the open-leg-stance *(Hachiji-Dachi)*. The punching hand begins at the waist in the upside-down position and travels

HELPFUL HINTS
Make sure the arms travel in a straight line. Keep the elbows tucked in.

in a straight line to the target. It stays relaxed, as does the rest of the body until just before the end of its travel, when it twists over (back of the fist up) and the body is tensed. The opposite arm pulls back at the same time and the fists twist over together. Contact is made with the Fore-fist *(Seiken)*.

How to apply *Choku-Zuki*

Stepping-Punch
Oi-Zuki

1 2 3 4

Forward Stance

A Stepping-punch *(Oi-Zuki)* is virtually the same as *Choku-Zuki* but performed whilst stepping forward or backwards. Starting from the downward-block *(Gedan-Barai)* position move the back leg forward so it comes close to the front leg, keeping them both bent at this point, and then carry on into the next Forward-stance *(Zenkutsu-Dachi)*.

The arms remain in almost the same position right until the end of the technique and then exchange places. At this point, the hips should be square on, muscles tensed and breath exhaled.

HELPFUL HINTS

As you change stance, try and move the stepping foot in a semi-circle.

How to apply *Oi-Zuki*

Reverse-Punch
Gyaku-Zuki

47

1 2 3 4

Forward Stance

HELPFUL HINTS
Think of the front hand grabbing and pulling

A Reverse-punch (Gyaku-Zuki) is a technique usually performed on the spot, using the reverse hand to punch with. It is possibly *Karate's* strongest punch, relying very much on using the power of the hips as they twist. From the Ready position *(Yoi)* in Forward-stance *(Zenkutsu-Dachi),* it is important to move both arms and hands at the same time. Keep the hips still in the 45° position and the body in the half-facing position *(Hanmi)* until the second half of the technique. As the right hand turns over to punch, so the left twists upside-down. At this point the right hip is thrust forward fully. The breath is exhaled and the body tensed. This final action of the hands, arms, hips, body, breathing and tension must all take place together.

How to apply
Gyaku-Zuki

Double-Punch
Morote-Zuki

1   2   3   4

Forward Stance

Double or Augmented punch *(Morote-Zuki)* begins with both hands upside-down at the waist. In this technique, both hands punch together. Either or both fists make contact - one punching, both punching, or one augmenting the other. On completion of this technique, both hips should remain fully-facing forward as the body is tensed and breath exhaled.

HELPFUL HINTS
Both hands and arms travel in a straight line to the target. Do **not** allow the elbows to protrude outwards.

How to apply *Morote-Zuki*

Rising-Punch
Age-Zuki

Forward Stance

Rising-punch *(Age-Zuki)* is a punch which makes use of the back of the fist and rises to contact the opponent under the chin. It is performed in a similar way to the reverse-punch, the main difference being, that the punching arm swings in a wide vertical arc. As the punch nears its completion, the reverse hip is thrust forward, the back leg tensed, as are the appropriate muscles used for this technique.

HELPFUL HINTS
It is important to be accurate when striking with this technique.

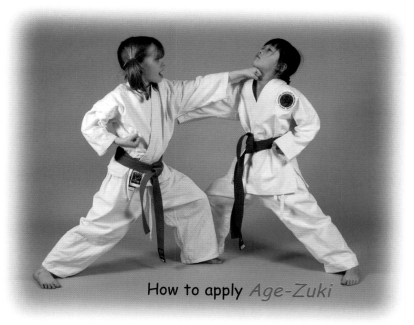

How to apply *Age-Zuki*

Roundhouse-Punch
Mawashi-Zuki

1 2 3 4

Forward Stance

Roundhouse-punch *(Mawashi-Zuki)* may be performed on the spot using the rear hand and hip, or as a stepping-punch depending on your distance from your attacker.

It follows an outward, circular rising path with the Fore-fist *(Seiken)* contacting the temple, at which time the hips should be rotated accordingly. The muscles should be tensed as you breathe out through your mouth.

HELPFUL HINTS
The punching arm should remain bent at all times.

How to apply *Mawashi-Zuki*

Close-Punch
Ura-Zuki

1   **2**   **3**

Forward Stance

Close-punch *(Ura-Zuki)* is a punch similar to *Gyaku-Zuki*, except the punching arm remains bent on completion and the fist upside-down. It travels in a straight line and the punch is complete when the punching arm elbow is about six inches from the hip. *Ura-Zuki* is an effective close in fighting technique when aimed at the Solar-Plexus.

HELPFUL HINTS
This is a short-range technique used very successfully when inside your opponent's defence.

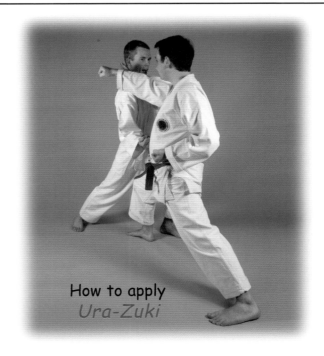

How to apply
Ura-Zuki

Vertical-Punch
Tate-Zuki

Forward Stance

A Vertical-punch *(Tate-Zuki)* is usually performed as a reverse *(gyaku)* technique similar again to *Gyaku-Zuki*. The same straight line is followed but this time, the fist turns only 90° - a quarter turn - and on completion, the punching arm remains bent at the elbow. Breathing and focus *(Kime)* are the same as preceding techniques.

HELPFUL HINTS

Contact is **not** made with the whole of the Fore-fist, only the front knuckles of the index and middle fingers.

How to apply *Tate-Zuki*

U-Punch
Yama-Zuki

1   **2**   **3**   **4**

Forward Stance

A U-punch *(Yama-Zuki)* is a multi-level attack (attacking two different areas at the same time). From a left forward-stance, put the right inverted fist by the waist and bring the left fist over the top of it, keeping it vertical.

HELPFUL HINTS
Both punches are to the centre of the body.

How to apply *Yama-Zuki*

From this beginning position, direct the right fist upward and forward in a semi-circular fashion towards the opponent's face. The right fist finishes with the back of the fist up, having turned 180°. The left fist pushes forward and, upside-down, attacks the solar-plexus. Both fists should reach the opponent together; therefore they should remain in a vertical line. A slight leaning forward of the body is normal.

Hook-Punch
Kage-Zuki

1　**2**　**3**　**4**

Straddle-Leg-Stance

A Hook-punch *(Kage-Zuki)* is ideal as a 'close-in-fighting' body punch where the fist finishes up in line with the body. It is necessary to step towards your opponent to ensure it is effective. Used a great deal in the *Tekki Kata*, this technique is usually performed in Straddle-leg-stance *(Kiba-Dachi)*. Special attention should be given to focus *(Kime)*, especially to the shoulders (Deltoids) and sides of the body (Latissimus Dorsi). (See 'Martin's Muscles' further on in this book).

HELPFUL HINTS

After blocking, sliding in to attack with Hook-Punch is a good move.

How to apply
Kage-Zuki

Punching

Quiz Time

What are the Japanese names for the following techniques?

Straight Punch.....................................

Reverse Punch.....................................

Rising Punch.....................................

Hook Punch.....................................

What is Fore-fist in Japanese?

....

Are all punches performed straight?

....

What is *'Hanmi'* in English?

....

Explain the word *'Kime'*

....

Blocking

It's a way of stopping a punch, strike or kick from hitting you. It leaves the person attacking unharmed and you then have the choice of hitting them back (counter-attacking) or not.

Think of it like this: For example, suppose someone was going to punch you in the face. Their fist would rise up from their waist towards your head. If you do nothing, the fist will hit you - not a good idea - is it?

So, we have to use our arms to stop it hitting us. We can strike or push the arm from underneath, pushing it over our head, or we can strike or push it sideways, so it misses our face. This is called deflecting; moving the punching arm to one side so the fist doesn't hit us. Clever, eh?

Having done this, we now have a choice. We are in charge or control of the situation. We can hit back, or walk away and do nothing.

The important thing is, we can choose what to do. As grown-ups would say, 'you are in the driving seat', and best of all, this person who wanted to punch you on the nose, failed to do so and all because of a good block. Wow!

Block in Japanese is *'Uke'*. Pronounced 'oo-kay'.

Downward-Block
Gedan-Barai

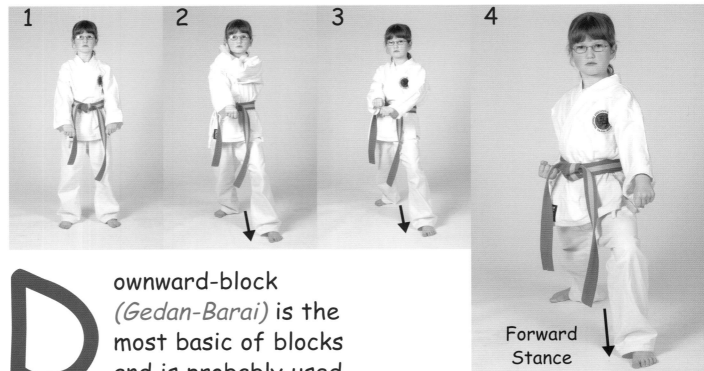

Forward Stance

Downward-block *(Gedan-Barai)* is the most basic of blocks and is probably used and practised more than any other *Karate* technique. Usually performed in *Zenkutsu-Dachi*, it makes maximum use of the arms, legs, body and hips. Most lessons involve many *Gedan-Barai's* - it's the first technique from the very first *Kata* and it's still there in the most advanced formal exercise. Yes; the left *Gedan-Barai* is most students' strongest block - but the right one - now that's a different matter.

HELPFUL HINTS
When bringing the fist to the opposite ear, the elbow must stay close to the chest.

How to apply
Gedan-Barai

Upper-Rising-Block
Age-Uke

1 2 3 4

Forward Stance

Upper-rising-block *(Age-Uke)* is one of the most basic *Shōtōkan* blocks. Points to remember are these: The blocking arm should rise from the waist at an angle of 45°. The arm and fist turn 180° at the end of the technique as contact is made. When pulling the opposite arm down, make sure the elbow pulls down in the direction of the hip. On completion, the hips and body must be 45° to the front and the back leg must be pushed almost straight on contact.

HELPFUL HINTS
Do not allow the blocking arm to lean back towards your fore-head.

How to apply
Age-Uke

Outside-Forearm-Block – Soto-Ude-Uke

Forward Stance

O utside-forearm-block *(Soto-Ude-Uke)* is perhaps the strongest mid-section block of all. On occasions it can be used to block kicks with surprising effectiveness. The block starts its life at *Jōdan* level pulled well back past the head. It travels from that position, in a semi-circle to a spot roughly in front of the chest and on completion, the wrist turns 180° just prior to *Kime*. Both body and hips turn into the half-facing position *(Hanmi)*.

HELPFUL HINTS

When raising the arm to block, have the elbow to the rear and the fist by the ear.

How to apply
Soto-Ude-Uke

Inside-Forearm-Block - Uchi-Ude-Uke

Forward Stance

I nside-forearm-block *(Uchi-Ude-Uke)* is a lot easier to perform than *Soto-Ude-Uke* as far as beginners are concerned. The blocking arm starts from above the opposite hip, back of the fist up and swings in an arc across the body. It finishes its journey in line with the side of the body, the elbow being bent at a 90° angle and the top of the fist in line with the shoulder. The body and hips twist to the 45° position as the block is completed.

HELPFUL HINTS
Halfway through this technique the body is square-on to the front. Twist into *Hanmi* as you block.

How to apply
Soto-Ude-Uke

Knife-Hand-Block
Shutō-Uke

1 2 3 4

Back Stance

Knife-hand-block (*Shutō-Uke*) is a technique more difficult than most, therefore it often gets neglected by beginners and high grades alike. Points to remember are: Keep the blocking arm at a 45° angle, otherwise, one may miss the punch completely. The opposite hand should strike the solar-plexus as it pulls back. This will assist in *Kime*. Keep the body and hips at 45° and try not to let the knees turn inwards.

HELPFUL HINTS
Keep the hands and fore-arms straight.

How to apply *Shutō-Uke*

Vertical-Knife-Hand-
Block - Tate-Shutō-Uke

Forward Stance

Vertical-knife-hand-block *(Tate-Shutō-Uke)* is a block using the knife-hand edge. One needs to be a little more confident when using this technique as opposed to the more conventional blocks. However, once the student has become reasonably accurate, this block will begin to appeal more. It can be used to attack inside or outside an opponent's arm and prepares the way for a rapid counter-attack.

HELPFUL HINTS
For the blocking hand to be vertical, that arm should be slightly bent at the elbow.

How to apply
Tate-Shutō-Uke

Upper-X-Block
Jōdan-Jūji-Uke

1   2   3   4

X Block *(Jūji-Uke)* is a very strong double-handed blocking technique that can be performed *Jōdan* or *Gedan*. In this, the *Jōdan* version, the hands rise from the hips at 45° and lock together, crossed above the head. The technique, shown here, is called *Haishū-Jūji-Uke*, for the back of the hands make contact with the attacker's arm. If performed from a left forward stance, it is important to have the right hip forward as the block concludes, with the left arm in front of the right. Correspondingly, when performed from a right stance, the right arm becomes the leading arm.

Forward Stance

HELPFUL HINTS
As you block, press the two hands together.

How to apply
Jōdan-Jūji-Uke

Lower-X-Block
Gedan-Jūji-Uke

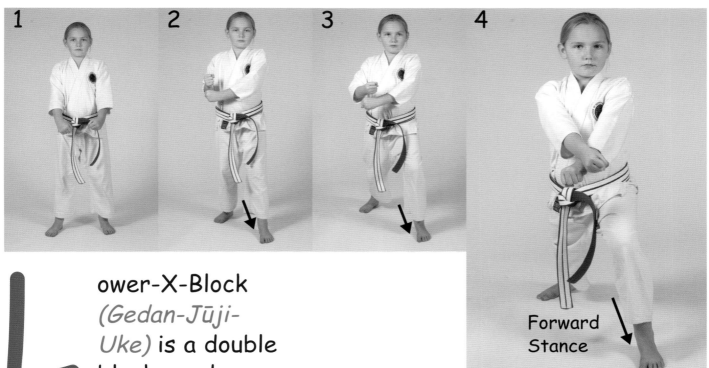

1   2   3   4

Forward Stance

Lower-X-Block *(Gedan-Jūji-Uke)* is a double block used together with the hips, to stop a front kick and simultaneously attack the shin-bone. It really consists of two techniques - Gedan-Barai and Tate-Zuki. To ensure success, this block needs to be executed quickly, stopping the kicking leg in its tracks and preventing it from gaining speed.

HELPFUL HINTS

On completion keep both hands locked together.

How to apply
Gedan-Jūji-Uke

Augmented-Forearm-Block Morote-Uke

1 **2** **3** **4**

Forward Stance

Augmented-forearm-block *(Morote-Uke)* is an inside-forearm-block augmented and strengthened by having the opposite arm assist it.

Indeed, the augmenting arm is quite interesting in so far as it hangs loosely by the side of the body, almost being left behind, then finally accelerates to catch the blocking arm up. In touching the blocking arm just inside the elbow it strengthens the block quite considerably, for it brings into play the muscles on that side of the body and promotes increased harmony.

HELPFUL HINTS

On completion, the body should be in *Hanmi* (Half-facing).

How to apply
Morote-Uke

Wedge-Block
Kakiwake-Uke

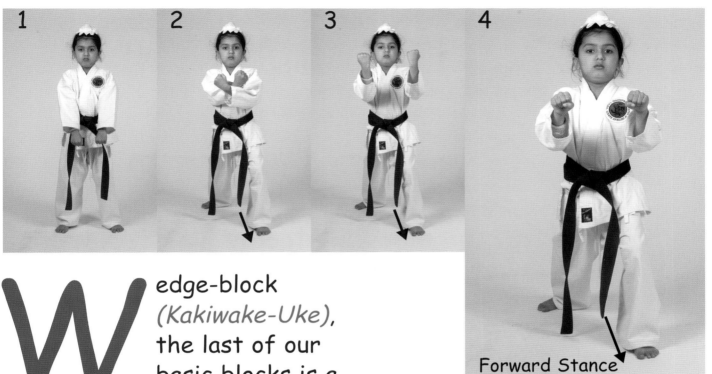

Forward Stance

Wedge-block *(Kakiwake-Uke)*, the last of our basic blocks is a disengagement technique (releasing) which, after training, is a very effective defence against being grabbed by the coat lapels. Its effective execution depends mainly on being able to tense the stomach *(Hara)* and the muscles at the side of the body. On completion, it leaves the attacker's body wide open and his position is extremely vulnerable (weak), having both hands and arms outside yours.

HELPFUL HINTS
Keep the chest and hips square on as the block is completed.

How to apply *Kakiwake-Uke*

Blocking Quiz Time

What are the Japanese names for the following techniques?

Downward-Block

....

Outside-Forearm-Block

....

Wedge-Block

....

Vertical-Knifehand-Block

....

What is a block?

....

What does *Shōtōkan* mean?

....

What does *Kiai* mean?

....

In *Shutō-Uke*, what part of the hand are you blocking with?............

How do you write 'X-Block' in Japanese? ....

Striking

A strike can be performed using different parts of the hand, foot, knee, elbow or head. For example: Instead of using the front of the fist as when practising a punch, the bottom or back of the fist may be used in a striking action.

There are many striking techniques using different parts of the open hand too. For example: The Knife-hand uses the edge of the hand (little finger side) and the Ridge-hand uses the thumb side. The Spear-hand, the tips of the first, second and third fingers, whilst the back of the hand may be used for striking.

The front, back and sides of the feet and elbows are also used to attack with, as is the back of the open hand.

All of the main strikes are covered in the following pages and learning them will be great fun.

Strike in Japanese is 'Uchi'. Pronounced 'oo-chee'.

Knife-Hand-Strike
Shutō-Uchi (Outside)

Knife-hand-strike *(Shutō-Uchi)* (outside) is a semi-circular strike to the neck or temple using the hand-edge or 'knife-hand'. As illustrated above it can be performed as a reverse technique, or as a stepping movement depending on distance *(Maai)*. In both cases proper use of the hips is essential.

HELPFUL HINTS
Keep the elbow slightly bent and the hand horizontal on completion.

How to apply *Shutō-Uke*

Knife-Hand-Strike
Shutō-Uchi (Inside)

Knife-hand-strike *(Shutō-Uchi)* (inside) uses the same part of the hand as the outside technique but commences its movement with the striking hand positioned by the opposite ear. The body should be twisted to a 45° angle *(Hanmi)* at the conclusion of the technique. Contact areas are the neck or temple.

HELPFUL HINTS

Don't lock the striking arm dead straight (to avoid elbow damage)

How to apply *Shutō-Uke*

Bottom-Fist-Strike
Tettsui-Uchi

Bottom-fist-strike *(Tettsui-Uchi)* can be used to attack most parts of the body. In the case of being grabbed by the wrist, one can use the swinging action of the arm to break the grip and continue over the head, so attacking the opponent's skull with *Tettsui-Uchi*. An obvious target area is the groin and in the case of the male, its vulnerable contents.

HELPFUL HINTS

This technique is sometimes referred to as Hammer-fist.

How to apply
Tettsui-Uchi

Back-Fist-Strike
Uraken-Uchi

Back-fist-strike *(Uraken-Uchi)* has basically two forms. The first employs a lateral, semi-circular snapping action focusing the back-fist on the opponent's temple. The second involves a semi-circular, overhead strike concentrating the power of the back-fist onto the opponent's nose. The former is a favourite technique for those involved in competitions, and tournaments, for the speed at which it can score can be devastating. A good example of the second occurs in the *Kata Heian Sandan.*

HELPFUL HINTS
The elbow acts as a fulcrum (pivot point) for the semi-circular movement.

How to apply *Uraken-Uchi*

Ridge-Hand-Strike
Haitō-Uchi (Outside)

Ridge-hand-strike *(Haitō-Uchi)* (outside) makes use of the opposite, thumb side, of the hand to *Shutō-Uchi.* The target area is the temple but make sure the thumb is not protruding out too far otherwise it may get broken. The striking hand swings round the body in a circular motion from a palm up to a palm down position. The beginner should understand straight line techniques before he attempts *Haitō-Uchi*, if not, he will allow his elbow to travel outside the body line when performing basic punches.

HELPFUL HINTS
Allow the striking arm elbow to travel outside the line of the body.

How to apply *Haitō-Uchi* (Outside)

Ridge-Hand-Strike
Haitō-Uchi (Inside)

Ridge-hand-strike *(Haitō-Uchi)* (inside) is often performed from the Straddle-leg-stance or as in the large photograph opposite, in Forward-stance *(Zenkutsu-Dachi)* The striking hand moves from palm down to the palm up position and the target area can be the face, temple or neck. On completion of this technique, the body is side-on to the opponent.

HELPFUL HINTS
The target area may be the temple, neck or throat.

How to apply *Haitō-Uchi* (Inside)

Upper-Elbow-Strike
Jōdan-Empi-Uchi

1 2 3 4

Forward Stance

Upper-elbow-strike *(Jōdan-Empi-Uchi)* is a strong effective *Karate* technique, however, the attacking range is drastically reduced when using elbow attacks as opposed to punches or strikes. Therefore *Empi* techniques are better for close encounters. On completion, the elbow should have contacted under the chin and have the back of the fist turned out. Good hip movement is important, and when the right arm does the striking, the right hip twists forward at the end of the technique.

HELPFUL HINTS
The striking point is the front of the elbow.

How to apply
Jōdan-Empi-Uchi

Middle-Elbow-Strike[77]
Chūdan-Empi-Uchi

1 **2** **3** **4**

Forward Stance

Middle-elbow-strike *(Chūdan-Empi-Uchi)* may be performed on the spot as a reverse *(gyaku)* technique or indeed practised as a stepping movement. Either way, the hip movement is of great importance and on completion the attackers index-finger knuckle of his striking hand should fit into the small of his chest (touching the sternum).

HELPFUL HINTS
The elbow travels in a semi-circular path.

How to apply *Chūdan-Empi-Uchi*

Middle-Back-Elbow-Strike
Chūdan-Ushiro-Empi-Uchi

Middle, back-elbow-strike (*Chūdan-Ushiro-Empi-Uchi*) is a formidable technique. When attacking in the reverse (*gyaku*) position as in the illustration, the left hip must be back as far as possible so aiding the

attacking elbow. The right hand assists for augmenting purposes. It is important to have the left fist facing palm up and the right hip pushed as far forward as possible. The beginner, when practising his first Straight-punch (*Choku-Zuki*), inadvertently (unknowingly) performs a back-elbow-strike.

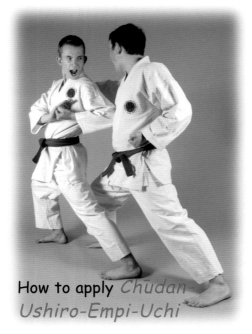

How to apply *Chūdan-Ushiro-Empi-Uchi*

Middle-Side-Elbow-Strike

Chdan-Yoko-Empi-Uchi

Middle-side-elbow-strike (*Chūdan-Yoko-Empi-Uchi*) is generally performed in the Straddle-leg-stance (*Kiba-Dachi*) and the opponent's sternum makes an adequate target for this penetrating technique. On completion, the back of the fist remains up and care should be taken to control very carefully when practising, as sternums have a nasty habit of breaking when hit by a *Yoko-Empi-Uchi*.

HELPFUL HINTS
Keep the forearm, not the upper arm in line with the target.

How to apply
Chūdan-Yoko-Empi-Uchi

Striking

Quiz Time

Name five strikes in Japanese..................................
Is it possible to strike with an elbow?...
Is there any connection between a strike in baseball and a *Karate* strike?...
Is it possible in *Karate* to strike with the finger tips?.......................
Name five areas of the hand used for striking...
What is *Uraken-Uchi?*.......................
Describe the action of an outside Ridge-hand-strike?................................
Why is the opposite hand important in any strike?................................
How do you write 'X-Block' in Japanese?...

Inside the Mind of a Child

The pupils of a Buckinghamshire School were asked one day if they had any 'heroes', and if so, would they care to write about them. Some days later, a letter arrived at my home. I opened it and took out the single sheet of paper. The envelope held nothing else. I had no idea where it had come from, or who had written it, not until I saw the boy's name at the bottom of the page.

As I read it, I was moved - considerably! It brought home to me the huge responsibility that teaching *Karate-dō* to children brings, and being privy to a child's crystallised thoughts was indeed a privilege. Being taught by a nine-year old *Karate* student was an unexpected learning experience, and put much into perspective, for which I'm grateful.

To Shihan

'You are the torch that guides me on the way.

You are the book that I learn from.

You are as helpful as a map.

You are like a farmer, watering his students till they grow to the top.

You are as defensive as a Panda for it's young.

Yet, you are as friendly as my dog.'

Jamie Locke

Kicking

As with punches, there are different kinds of kicks and they use different parts of the foot to attack with. There are front-kicks, back-kicks, side-kicks and round-kicks.

Of course, kicking uses the legs and feet and because the legs are bigger and stronger than the arms, kicks usually are more powerful.

The first kick taught is the Front-kick and is included in the examination for the first belt. As you go higher in grade, so other kicks are introduced.

Kicks are difficult to master and need a lot of practice. They are however, exciting, can be great fun (unless you are on the receiving end of one) and when performed correctly, give great satisfaction. The main kicks needed up to black belt are shown on the following pages.

Kick in Japanese is *Keri*, but when joined by another word becomes *Geri*. For example: *Mae-Geri* (front-kick), *Yoko-Geri* (side-kick), and so on. For *geri* just say (geh-rhee).

Front-Kick
Mae-Geri

A Front-kick (*Mae-Geri*) performed from a Forward-stance (*Zenkutsu-Dachi*) is a snap-kick acquiring its power from the snapping action of the lower leg aided by the application of the hips. Basically there are three positions that make-up this kick. Firstly, the kicking leg knee is raised in front and to the centre of the body. Secondly, the leg is almost straightened, hips applied, instep straightened and toes curled back. Thirdly, the lower leg is snapped back assuming the first position and with the hips returned to their original position, the back should be straight and balance maintained.

HELPFUL HINTS
When kicking, think more of pushing the opposite hip forward.

How to apply *Mae-Geri*

Side-Snap-Kick
Yoko-Geri-Keage

1 **2** **3** **4**

Side-snap-kick *(Yoko-Geri-Keage)* is another snap-kick but this time the kicking leg travels to the side of the body. Usually performed from a Straddle-leg-stance *(Kiba-Dachi)*, the kicking leg knee is first raised to the side, then the leg is straightened and at this point, the hip rises up to augment the snapping action. Finally, the leg is snapped back, hip lowered and the stance resumed. The striking point is the foot-edge *(Sokuto)*.

HELPFUL HINTS
Pivot on the ball of the supporting foot.

How to apply *Yoko-Geri-Keage*

Side-Thrust-Kick
Yoko-Geri-Kekomi

Side-thrust-kick *(Yoko-Geri-Kekomi)* utilizes the thrusting action of the leg augmented by the hip. It is more of a 'total commitment' technique and requires good control and balance keeping the recovery factor in mind. As with *Yoko-Geri-Keage,* the striking point is the foot edge *(Sokuto).* An important point to bear in mind is the pivoting action on the ball of the supporting foot as the thrusting takes place. Failure to do this could result in a damaged cartilage in the knee of that supporting leg.

HELPFUL HINTS
Thrust the hip forward in the direction of the target.

How to apply
Yoko-Geri-Kekomi

Roundhouse-Kick
Mawashi-Geri

A Roundhouse-kick *(Mawashi-Geri)* is a semi-circular snap-kick using the ball of the foot *(Koshi)* as the striking point. From a Forward-stance *(Zenkutsu-Dachi)*, raise the knee sideways keeping the leg bent and the toes curled up. Then snap the leg forward aiming the foot at the target, at the same time allowing the hips to rotate. Immediately the leg has straightened, snap it back together with the hips to their original position. At all times endeavour to keep the knee of the kicking leg higher than the foot.

HELPFUL HINTS
Jōdan targets are the neck and temple.

How to apply
Mawashi-Geri

Reverse-Kick
Ushiro-Geri

Reverse-kick *(Ushiro-Geri)* makes use of the thrusting action of the leg, aided by the hips in a rearward direction. Often performed as a spinning technique using the heel as a striking point, *Ushiro-Geri* takes the face of the person kicking furthest away from the attacker and encourages him to commit himself to the technique much more. However, this commitment in competitions may result in disqualification through excessive contact. Both hips should be thrust back together, similar to *Oi-Zuki* or *Mae-Geri*, but in reverse.

HELPFUL HINTS
On contact keep the foot vertical (toes down).

How to apply
Ushiro-Geri

Crescent-Kick-Block
Mikazuki-Geri-Uke

1 **2** **3** **4**

Crescent-kick-block *(Mikazuki-Geri-Uke)* may be used as a block or an attack using the sole of the foot as a striking point.

Endeavour to keep the knee parallel to the floor when performing this semi-circular movement.

HELPFUL HINTS
An excellent technique that is practised very little with the right leg and never with the left.

How to apply
Mikazuki-Geri-Uke

Crescent-Kick
Mikazuki-Geri

A Crescent-kick-block (*Mikazuki-Geri*) performed as a block or an attack utilises the ball of the foot *(koshi)*. The kick takes its name from the crescent like action of the leg, whether moving in an inward or outward direction. The thigh of the kicking leg should remain parallel to the floor if possible.

HELPFUL HINTS
This technique should be practised with both legs as *Heian Godan* and *Bassai-Dai* involve only a right one.

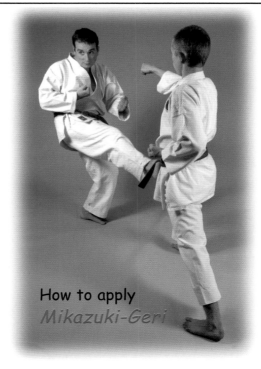

How to apply
Mikazuki-Geri

Back-Roundhouse-Kick *Ushiro-Mawashi-Geri*

Back-Roundhouse-kick *(Ushiro-Mawashi-Geri)* differs from *Mawashi-Geri* in that the kicking leg travels in a reverse direction, swinging in a reverse arc allowing the lower leg to snap back using the heel to strike the target. Pivot on the front foot when using it as a spinning kick.

HELPFUL HINTS

In competition, the sole of the foot is often used to make contact with.

How to apply
Ushiro-Mawashi-Geri

Kicking Quiz Time

Name five kicks in Japanese

....

Name five kicks in English

....

What part of the foot does *Yoko-Geri-Keage* use to contact with?

....

In a Front-Kick, should the toes be pointed or curled up?

....

Name a kick where both hips should be forward on contact

....

What is the difference between a snap-kick and a thrust-kick?

....

Kata - It's like a bus route

'Simply put, it's *Karate* moves practised in a pattern. Not clear? Ok - well, imagine different *Karate* movements performed in a set direction. Still not clear?

Well think of it like this: A *Kata* is like a bus route. The driver has to drive his bus along a set route. He is not allowed to alter or change it by driving off-route up a back street, because all the people waiting at the bus-stops are on his route, and they know he will arrive at a certain time at their bus-stop.

So, think of yourself as the bus driver. When you are practising *Kata*, you are the bus driver and must follow exactly the same route or pattern every time. Just as the bus driver's driving ability improves, so your techniques in *Kata* become sharper, stronger and faster.

The more you practise, the better you will become. Soon, you won't have to think of the techniques or the direction in which to perform them.

You will just do them! I guess the word is - automatically.

Now jump in your bus, and lets go! The first route or pattern is *Taikyoku-Shodan* - and it's great fun!'

Sensei - tell me more about Kata

Sensei, go on, tell us a story about *Kata* - please...

Looking down at the young student who had asked the question, *Sensei* paused for just a moment. 'Now let me see...

Once-upon-a-time, more than one thousand years ago in China, lived an old man. For more than forty-years he had lived alone, high up in the rugged mountains of the Northern Province of Chang Shi. He was a martial artist and had been so for as long as he could remember.

His teacher had died many years earlier in the great earthquake that split his province in two and left him without friends or family.

With a heavy heart, he headed for higher ground and isolation with only his martial art for comfort.

On odd occasions he would meet monks on their

travels across China, and he would invite them to spend a few days with him as his guests. He really looked forward to these times as they were the only occasions when he met other human beings.

The monks would teach him self-defence techniques in return for instruction in his fighting art. When they left, he would practise the techniques from dawn till dusk, as he returned to his lonely and isolated life in the mountains. Fortunately, he had a wonderful imagination, which helped enormously, as most of the time he practised alone, fighting off countless imaginary opponents.

Over the years, he developed almost fifty patterns for his imaginary opponents to attack in. This enabled him to create as many patterns (or *Kata*) of his own to deal with the attackers depending on how they attacked, with what, and from which direction they came from.

On his lonely mountain top he devised a simple model for all his martial arts movements to be performed on imaginary attackers. It was both simple yet ingenious, and the design resembled the modern day compass.

He realised, any attack could only come from one of eight directions. There was no room for any more!

Today, all *Kata* (formal exercise) when being performed, have imaginary attackers approaching from just eight directions. *Kata* is quite remarkable and has so many benefits, most of which you'll learn

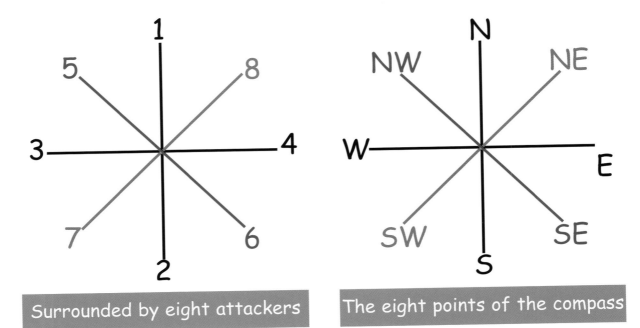

Surrounded by eight attackers

The eight points of the compass

of later in Volume 2.'

The innocent young student looked up at his teacher. 'Sensei, is this story of the old man true - or is it one of your made-up ones?'

Sensei paused again, he seemed to be miles away. 'Well', he said, 'It could be true, or it could indeed be one that I made up. I'll leave that for you to decide.

Just use your imagination every day, and as you grow up, you'll never lose it.

If you stop, it will disappear, and unfortunately, it seldom returns.' The young boy bowed deeply, for he knew there was a message in Sensei's story just for him.

That night, as he lay in his bed, he imagined what it would be like to be a man. Suddenly he was surrounded and being attacked by eight opponents. His blocks and counter-attacks were strong and as fast as lightning - they stood no chance.

It was as if he knew where each attack was coming from.

He smiled, turned, and walked away, and as he did so - he fell fast asleep.

Sparring –

Training with a partner

Ask any class of young boys, 'who wants to learn how to fight?' and you'll be faced with a sea of hands and cries of 'Me! Me! Me!'

With sparring *(Kumite)*, the time has now come to see if those blocks you have been practising constantly, really work.

If they don't, we could be in for a few tears.

There are many types of sparring that eventually lead on to free-sparring. The secret is to practise your basics until they become second nature.

'Second nature! What's that?', I hear you say.

'Well. Think of it like this.

Do you have to think about breathing in and out? Of course you don't, you do it all the time - it's second nature.

When you go to sleep at night-time, do you have to remember to carry on breathing all night? Of course not, that's second nature too, as everything is you practise often enough. Walking is a very good example. You don't have to think about putting your left foot in front of your right and visa versa. You do it without thinking, for you've done it so often, it's become second nature.

In *Karate*, if you practise your basics enough, they will in time become second nature too. When you are attacked in sparring by someone using a punch to the head, you will automatically defend with an upper rising block. You won't have to think, what block shall I use? You'll just select the right one. It will have become s----- n-----. I'm sure you can fill in the spaces - can't you?'

What should you do if you meet a bully?

This can be a difficult one.

To find the answer it may be helpful to understand his motivation. What makes him the way he is. What has happened in his life to make him behave in such a way. Bullies are usually cowards, and they don't like getting hurt. This is probably the main reason for them going around in groups.

A lone wolf is not too brave, but in a pack he's a different animal!

So why does a bully act this way?

It may go back to his childhood where he may have been beaten or abused, or treated badly in some other way by parents, relatives or 'friends'.

He most certainly suffers from insecurity and a lack of confidence. He is trying to show others by his actions that he is not scared, is tough, confident and in control. By attempting to dominate, he exhibits exactly the opposite.

Some years ago, my son Mansel was confronted continuously at school by a bigger lad who was nothing more than an out and out bully. It transpired, the reason he and his 'chums' didn't like Mansel, was because he had previously been to a boarding school near Bourne in Lincolnshire. As a result he spoke a shade differently to his peers at this Northamptonshire state school and subsequently became the centre of ridicule.

The bully approached Mansel on numerous occasions wanting to fight him. Mansel tried to reason with him by telling him he didn't want to fight - he had nothing against him, and further more, he thought fighting was stupid, with a distinct possibility of getting hurt.

One evening Mansel came to talk with me and explained the current situation. He wanted some advice. It was obviously becoming a problem and affecting his studies.

I explained to him that sometimes in life, it's necessary to confront certain people head-on, and call their bluff. I suggested an appropriate course of action, even so, it was a trifle risky.

Pick your moment and inform the bully you have decided to take him up on his offer of a fight and will meet him by himself after school, at four o'clock tomorrow in the church-yard. The bully was taken aback, but agreed to the rendezvous. The church-yard was the perfect venue as it lay opposite our house, and without telling Mansel, I concealed myself in the bushes, just in case the bully brought his gang for additional support.

At 3.50 pm, Mansel arrived at the church-yard and waited. I looked at my watch - it was 4.02pm and no sign of the bully. At 4.10pm he came around the corner and approaching Mansel, stopped some twenty metres away. He was alone. As he spoke, I detected a noticeable tremor in his voice.

'Mansel, do you really want to fight? I know I don't. Let's shake hands and be friends.'

It was music to Mansel's ears. 'Of course I don't want to fight - I kept telling you that.'

Mansel walked over and shook the bully's moist hand.

Both boys smiled, with a promise of seeing each other the following day at school.

In the two years that followed, Mansel has had no trouble whatsoever with any of his peers, before heading for university in Pembrokeshire.

Postscript: To this day, he never knew I was positioned in the undergrowth. The first he will know about it will be when he reads this book. I know it won't be a problem.

Mansel shakes hands with the bully

YOU ARE WHAT YOU EAT!

The object of this chapter is to make you more aware of what foods you are putting into your mouth and whether they are good or bad for you.

You are probably between the ages of five and twelve, so I'm going to ask you one more question. Wouldn't it be sensible for say the next fifty years, to only put good food into your body? Of course it would.

By doing this, you will become so much healthier and you will probably stand a good chance of avoiding many of the illnesses that people get, like cancer.

Should you carry on with your *Karate* training, as I hope you will, becoming fitter both in mind and body will happen quite naturally. By training in *Karate* and eating a correct balanced diet, you can make your body the size and shape you want it to be - wow!

It's easy to do, and school meals are changing for the better, largely thanks to TV chef Jamie Oliver.

Good	Bad
Fruit-Vegetables-Meat-Poultry-Fish-Cereals-Whole-meal Bread-Eggs-Milk-Fruit-Juices-Pasta-Salads	Sugar-Fat-Oil-Butter-Chips-Junk-food-Cakes-Biscuits-Chocolate-Sweets-Coke Cola-Fizzy Drinks-Crisps-Doughnuts-Cream

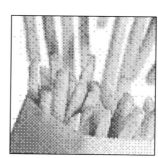

The Dōjō Kun

Morals of the training hall

To the best of my knowledge, *The Dōjō Kun* was first recited in the UK on a Tuesday evening in December 1966, at St. Michael's church hall in Enfield, North London.

I had the honour of bringing it from Japan for I felt it elevated *Karate* from being a physical pursuit, into a way of life with huge mental and spiritual connotations. Living *The Dōjō Kun* is probably *Karate-dō's* greatest challenge. It is the ultimate test to which few aspire.

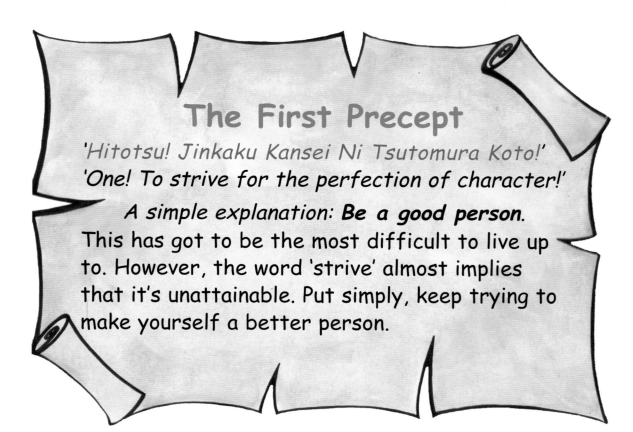

The First Precept

'Hitotsu! Jinkaku Kansei Ni Tsutomura Koto!'

'One! To strive for the perfection of character!'

A simple explanation: **Be a good person.** This has got to be the most difficult to live up to. However, the word 'strive' almost implies that it's unattainable. Put simply, keep trying to make yourself a better person.

'When there is one eye fixed upon your destination, there is only one eye left with which to find the way.'

The Second Precept

'Hitotsu! Makoto No Michi O Mamoru Koto!'

'One! To defend the paths of truth!'

A simple explanation:

Do what is right.

Always try to do the right thing. Be on the side of truth and right and support them both to the best of your ability.

The Third Precept

'Hitotsu! Doryoku No Seishin O Yashinau Koto!'

'One! To foster the spirit of effort!'

A simple explanation:

Don't ever give up.

Keep trying. Develop your ability to remain steadfast, especially in times of adversity.

The Fourth Precept

'Hitotsu! Reigi O Omonzuru Koto!'

'One! To honour the principles of etiquette!'

A simple explanation:

Be polite.

Always exercise good manners. Respect others. Appreciate having been given the rules of good human conduct. Consider others first.

The Fifth Precept

'Hitotsu! Kekki No Yu O Imashimuru Koto!'

'One! To guard against impetuous courage!'

A simple explanation:

Think before you act.

Consider all circumstances before taking a course of action. Be careful not to act impulsively.

The Eleven Steps on the ladder to Black Belt

Grade	Colour of belt
Beginner	White belt
10th Kyu	Blue belt
9th Kyu	Red belt
8th Kyu	Orange belt
7th Kyu Intermediate	Orange with 1 yellow stripe
7th Kyu	Yellow belt
6th Kyu Intermediate	Yellow with 1 green stripe
6th Kyu	Green belt
5th Kyu Intermediate	Green with 1 purple stripe
5th Kyu	Purple belt
4th Kyu Intermediate	Purple with 1 white stripe
4th Kyu	Purple with 2 white stripes
3rd Kyu Intermediate	Purple with 1 brown stripe
3rd Kyu	Brown belt
2nd Kyu Intermediate	Brown with 1 white stripe
2nd Kyu	Brown with 2 white stripes
1st Kyu Intermediate	Brown with 1 red stripe
1st Kyu	Brown with 2 red stripes
1st Dan Intermediate	Brown with 1 black stripe
1st Dan (Shodan)	Black belt

The eight intermediate grades are for juniors under the age of 14 years. The intermediate grade syllabus is the same as for the next higher grade but only the first half of the Kata is required.

The Journey Begins...

The following grading syllabus has been used successfully for the past thirty-years (with minor amendments) by *The Traditional Association of Shōtōkan Karate (TASK)*. Many Karate associations have adopted it, both here in the UK and abroad, and should any other group wish to use it, they are most welcome to do so.

Blue belt - 10th Kyu

Technique	Stance	No.	Additional information
Choku-Zuki (Straight-punch)	Shizentai (Natural-stance)	10	Facing forward
Gyaku-Zuki (Reverse-punch)	Zenkutsu-Dachi (Forward-stance)	5	Left side and right side
Oi-Zuki (Stepping-punch)	Zenkutsu-Dachi (Forward-stance)	3	Stepping forward, turn in Downward-block-repeat
Age-Uke (Upper-rising-block)	Zenkutsu-Dachi (Forward-stance)	3	Stepping forward, turn in Downward-block-repeat
Uchi-Ude-Uke (Inside-forearm-block)	Zenkutsu-Dachi (Forward-stance)	3	Stepping forward, turn in Downward-block-repeat
Gedan-Barai (Downward-block)	Zenkutsu-Dachi (Forward-stance)	3	Stepping forward, turn in Downward-block-repeat
Mae-Geri (Front-kick)	Zenkutsu-Dachi (Forward-stance)	3	Stepping forward, turn both arms down-repeat
Kata (**Formal-exercise**)	Taikyoku Shodan		First half only-to count
Kumite (**Sparring**)	None		

Red Belt –
9th Kyu

Technique	Stance	No.	Additional information
Kihon (Basics)			
Choku-Zuki (Straight-punch)	Shizentai (Natural-stance)	10	Facing forward
Gyaku-Zuki (Reverse-punch)	Zenkutsu-Dachi (Forward-stance)	5	Left side and right side
Oi-Zuki (Stepping-punch)	Zenkutsu-Dachi (Forward-stance)	3	Stepping forward, turn in Downward-block-repeat
Age-Uke (Upper-rising-block)	Zenkutsu-Dachi (Forward-stance)	3	Stepping forward, turn in Downward-block-repeat
Soto-Ude-Uke (Outside-forearm-block)	Zenkutsu-Dachi (Forward-stance)	3	Stepping forward, turn in Downward-block-repeat
Uchi-Ude-Uke (Inside-forearm-block)	Zenkutsu-Dachi (Forward-stance)	3	Stepping forward, turn in Downward-block-repeat
Gedan-Barai (Downward-block)	Zenkutsu-Dachi (Forward-stance)	3	Stepping forward, turn in Downward-block-repeat
Mae-Geri (Front-kick)	Zenkutsu-Dachi (Forward-stance)	3	Stepping forward, turn both arms down-repeat
Kumite **(Sparring)**	Gohon Kumite (5 Attack Sparring)		Jōdan (upper) - no count
Kata **(Formal-exercise)**	Taikyoku Shodan		Complete Kata - fast no count

Orange Belt – 8th Kyu

Technique	Stance	No.	Additional information
Kihon (Basics)			
Choku-Zuki (Straight-punch)	Shizentai (Natural-stance)	10	Facing forward
Gyaku-Zuki (Reverse-punch)	Zenkutsu-Dachi (Forward-stance)	5	Left side and right side
Oi-Zuki (Stepping-punch)	Zenkutsu-Dachi (Forward-stance)	3	Stepping forward and backwards
Age-Uke (Upper-rising-block)	Zenkutsu-Dachi (Forward-stance)	3	Stepping forward and backwards
Soto-Ude-Uke (Outside-forearm-block)	Zenkutsu-Dachi (Forward-stance)	3	Stepping forward and backwards
Uchi-Ude-Uke (Inside-forearm-block)	Zenkutsu-Dachi (Forward-stance)	3	Stepping forward and backwards
Gedan-Barai (Downward-block)	Zenkutsu-Dachi (Forward-stance)	3	Stepping forward and backwards
Mae-Geri (Front-kick)	Zenkutsu-Dachi (Forward-stance)	3	Stepping forward, turn both arms down-repeat
Shutō-Uke (Knife-hand-block)	Kōkutsu-Dachi (Back-stance)	3	Stepping forward and backwards
Yoko-Geri-Keage (Side-snap-kick)	Kiba-Dachi (Straddle-leg-stance)	3	Stepping forward, turn, same back
Yoko-Geri-Kekomi (Side-thrust-kick)	Kiba-Dachi (Straddle-leg-stance)	3	Stepping forward, turn, same back
Kumite (Sparring)	Gohon Kumite (5 Attack Sparring)		Jōdan and Chūdan no count
Kata (Formal-exercise)	Heian Shodan		Plus any previous Kata

Yellow Belt - 7th Kyu

Technique	Stance	No.	Additional information
Kihon (Basics)			
Oi-Zuki (Stepping-punch)	Zenkutsu-Dachi (Forward-stance)	3	Stepping forward and backwards
Age-Uke/Gyaku-Zuki (Upper-rising-block/Reverse-punch)	Zenkutsu-Dachi (Forward-stance)	3	Stepping forward and backwards
Soto-Ude-Uke/ Gyaku-Zuki (Outside-forearm-block/Reverse-punch)	Zenkutsu-Dachi (Forward-stance)	3	Stepping forward and backwards
Uchi-Ude-Uke/ Gyaku-Zuki (Inside-forearm-block/ Reverse-punch)	Zenkutsu-Dachi (Forward-stance)	3	Stepping forward and backwards
Shutō-Uke/Nukite (Knife-hand-block/Spear hand-thrust)	Kōkutsu-Dachi (Back stance) Zenkutsu-Dachi (Forward-stance)	3	Stepping forward and backwards
Mae-Geri (Front-kick)	Zenkutsu-Dachi (Forward-stance)	3	Stepping forward, turn, both arms down, repeat
Yoko-Geri-Keage (Side-snap-kick)	Kiba-Dachi (Straddle-leg-stance)	3	Stepping forward, turn, same back
Yoko-Geri-Kekomi (Side-thrust-kick)	Kiba Dachi (Straddle-leg-stance)	3	Stepping forward, turn same back
Kumite (Sparring)	Kihon-Ippon-Kumite (1-attack-sparring)		Set 1 Attack Jōdan, Chūdan and Mae-Geri (both sides)
Kata (Formal-exercise)	Heian Nidan		Plus any previous Kata

Green Belt - 6th Kyu

Technique	Stance	No.	Additional informatio
Kihon (Basics)			
Sanbon-Zuki (Stepping-3-punches)	*Zenkutsu-Dachi* (Forward-stance)	3	Stepping forward, turn and same back
Age-Uke/Gyaku-Zuki/Gedan-Barai (Upper-rising-block/Reverse-punch/Downward-block)	*Zenkutsu-Dachi* (Forward-stance)	3	Stepping forward and backwards
Uchi-Ude-Uke/Gyaku-Zuki/Gedan-Barai (Inside-forearm-block/ Reverse-punch/ Downward-block)	*Zenkutsu-Dachi* (Forward-stance)	3	Stepping forward and backwards
Shutō-Uke/Mae-Kizami-Geri/Nukite (Knife-hand-block/Front-leg-front-kick/Spear-hand-thrust)	*Kōkutsu-Dachi* (Back-stance) *Zenkutsu-Dachi* (Forward-stance)	3	Stepping forward and backwards
Ren-Mae-Geri (*Jōdan/ Chūdan*) (Double-front-kick (upper and middle))	*Zenkutsu-Dachi* (Forward-stance)	3	Turn, same back but *Chūdan/Jōdan*
Yoko-Geri-Keage (Side-snap-kick)	*Kiba-Dachi* (Straddle-leg-stance)	3	Stepping forward, turn, same back
Yoko-Geri-Kekomi (Side-thrust-kick)	*Kiba Dachi* (Straddle-leg-stance)	3	Stepping forward, turn same back
Mawashi-Geri (Roundhouse-kick)	*Zenkutsu-Dachi* (Forward-stance)	3	Stepping forward, turn same back
Kumite **(Sparring)**	*Kihon-Ippon-Kumite* (1-attack-sparring)		Set 2 Attack *Jōdan*, *Chūdan*, *Mae-Geri* both sides
Kata **(Formal-exercise)**	*Heian Sandan*		Plus any previous *Kata*

Purple Belt –
5th Kyu

Technique	Stance	No.	Additional information
Kihon (Basics)			
Sanbon-Zuki (Stepping-3-punches)	Zenkutsu-Dachi (Forward-stance)	3	Stepping forward, turn and same back
Age-Uke/Mae-Geri/ Gyaku-Zuki (Upper-rising-block/Front-kick/Reverse-punch)	Zenkutsu-Dachi (Forward-stance)	3	Stepping forward and Backwards
Uchi-Ude-Uke/ Kizami-Zuki/Gyaku-Zuki (Inside-forearm-block/ Jabbing-punch/Reverse-punch)	Zenkutsu-Dachi (Forward-stance)	3	Stepping forward and Backwards
Shutō-Uke/Mae-Kizami-Geri/Nukite (Knife-hand-block/Front-leg-front-kick/Spear-hand-thrust)	Kōkutsu-Dachi (Back-stance) Zenkutsu-Dachi (Forward-stance)	3	Stepping forward and Backwards
Mae-Geri/Oi-Zuki (Front-kick/Stepping-punch)	Zenkutsu-Dachi (Forward-stance)	3	Turn, Mae-Geri/Gyaku-Zuki (Front-kick/Reverse-punch).
Ren-Mae-Geri(Jōdan/Chūdan) (Double-front-kick (upper and middle))	Zenkutsu-Dachi (Forward-stance)	3	Turn, same back but Chūdan/Jōdan
Ren-Geri. Mae-Geri Mawashi-Geri Double-kick: Front and Round-house-kicks)	Zenkutsu-Dachi (Forward-stance)	3	Turn, same back but Mawashi-Geri/Mae-Geri
Ren-Geri: Mae-Geri/Yoko-Geri-Kekomi (Double-kick: Front-kick/ Side-thrust-kick)	Zenkutsu-Dachi (Forward-stance)	3	Turn, Yoko-Geri-Kekomi/ Mae-Geri
Kumite (Sparring)	Kihon-Ippon-Kumite (1-attack-sparring)		Set 3 Attack, Jōdan, Chūdan, Mae-Geri, Kekomi and Mawashi-Geri both sides.
Kata (Formal-exercise)	Heian Yondan		Plus any previous Kata

Purple Belt - 4th Kyu

With 2 white stripes

Technique	Stance	No.	Additional information
Kihon (**Basics**)			
Sanbon-Zuki	*Zenkutsu-Dachi*	5	Stepping forward, turn *Mae-Geri/Sanbon-Zuki*
Age-Uke/Mae-Geri/ Gyaku-Zuki/Gedan-Barai	*Zenkutsu-Dachi*	5	Stepping forward and backwards
Soto-Ude-Uke/ Yoko-Empi-Uchi/ Jōdan-Uraken-Uchi/ Chūdan-Gyaku-Zuki/ Gedan-Barai	*Zenkutsu-Dachi Kiba-Dachi Kiba-Dachi Zenkutsu-Dachi Zenkutsu-Dachi*	5	Stepping forward and backwards
Uchi-Ude-Uke/ Kizami-Zuki/Gyaku-Zuki/Gedan-Barai	*Kōkutsu-Dachi Zenkutsu-Dachi Zenkutsu-Dachi*	5	Stepping forward and backwards
Shutō-Uke/ Mae-Kizami-Geri/ Nukite	*Kōkutsu-Dachi Zenkutsu-Dachi*	5	Stepping forward and backwards
Mae-Geri/Mawashi-Geri/Jōdan-Uraken-Uchi/Chūdan-Gyaku-Zuki/Gedan-Barai	*Zenkutsu-Dachi*	3	Turn, same back
Mae-Geri/Yoko-Geri Kekomi/Jōdan-Shutō-Uchi/Chūdan-Gyaku-Zuki/Gedan-Barai	*Zenkutsu-Dachi*	3	Turn, same back
Yoko-Geri-Keage/ Chūdan-Gyaku-Zuki/ Gedan-Barai	*Kiba-Dachi Zenkutsu-Dachi Kiba-Dachi*	3	Turn, same back
Kumite (**Sparring**)	*Kihon-Ippon-Kumite*		Set 4. Attack, *Jōdan, Chūdan, Mae Geri, Kekomi* and *Mawashi-Ge* both sides
Kata (**Formal-exercise**)	*Heian Godan*		Plus any previous *Kata*

Brown Belt –
3rd Kyu

Technique	Stance	No.	Additional information
Kihon **(Basics)**			
Sanbon-Zuki	*Zenkutsu-Dachi*	5	Stepping forward, turn *Mae-Geri/Sanbon-Zuki*
Age-Uke/Mae-Geri/ Gyaku-Zuki/Gedan-Barai	*Zenkutsu-Dachi*	5	Stepping forward and backwards
Soto-Ude-Uke/ Yoko-Empi-Uchi/ Jōdan-Uraken-Uchi/ Chūdan-Gyaku-Zuki/ Gedan-Barai	*Zenkutsu-Dachi Kiba-Dachi Kiba-Dachi Zenkutsu-Dachi Zenkutsu-Dachi*	5	Stepping forward and backwards
Uchi-Ude-Uke/ Kizami-Zuki/Gyaku-Zuki/ Gedan-Barai	*Kōkutsu-Dachi Zenkutsu-Dachi Zenkutsu-Dachi*	5	Stepping forward and backwards
Shutō-Uke/ Mae-Kizami-Geri/Nukite	*Kōkutsu-Dachi Zenkutsu-Dachi*	5	Stepping forward and backwards
Mae-Geri/Mawashi Geri/ Jōdan-Uraken-Uchi/ Chūdan-Gyaku-Zuki/ Gedan-Barai	*Zenkutsu-Dachi*	3	Turn, same back
Mae-Geri/Yoko-Geri-Kekomi/ Jōdan-Shutō-Uchi Chūdan-Gyaku-Zuki/ Gedan-Barai	*Zenkutsu-Dachi*	3	Turn, same back
Yoko-Geri-Keage/ Chūdan-Gyaku-Zuki/ Gedan-Barai	*Kiba-Dachi Zenkutsu-Dachi Kiba-Dachi*	3	Turn, same back
Ushiro-Geri	*Zenkutsu-Dachi*	3	Turn, same back

Facing the front in *Zenkutsu Dachi*, kick *Mae-Geri* forward and *Yoko-Geri-Kekomi* to the side with the same leg. Repeat from opposite stance with other back leg.

3rd Kyu Continued

Technique	Stance	No.	Additional information
Kumite **(Sparring)**	Kihon-Ippon-Kumite (1-attack-sparring) Jiyū-Ippon-Kumite (Semi-free-1-attack-sparring)		Set 5. Attack, Jōdan, Chūdan, Mae-geri, Kekomi, Mawashi-Geri both sides Set 1. Attack with right side only, Jōdan, Chūdan and Mae-Geri
Kata **(Formal exercise)**	Tekki Shodan		Plus any previous Kata

Brown Belt - 2nd Kyu

With 2 white stripes

Technique	Stance	No.	Additional information
Kumite **(Sparring)**	Kihon-Ippon-Kumite (1-attack-sparring) Jiyū-Ippon-Kumite (Semi-free-1-attack-sparring)		Any set of the examiners choice. Attack from both sides Set 2. Attack from both sides with Jōdan, Chūdan and Mae-Geri
Kata **(Formal exercise)**	Bassai-Dai		Plus any previous Kata

Brown Belt - 2nd Kyu

Continued

Technique	Stance	No.	Additional information
Kihon (**Basics**)			
Sanbon-Zuki	*Zenkutsu-Dachi*	5	Stepping forward, turn *Mae-Geri/Sanbon-Zuki*
Age-Uke/Mae-Geri/ Gyaku-Zuki/Gedan-Barai	*Zenkutsu-Dachi*	5	Stepping forward and backwards
Soto-Ude-Uke/ Yoko-Empi-Uchi/ Jōdan-Uraken-Uchi/ Chūdan-Gyaku-Zuki/ Gedan-Barai	*Zenkutsu-Dachi Kiba-Dachi Kiba-Dachi Zenkutsu-Dachi Zenkutsu-Dachi*	5	Stepping forward and backwards
Uchi-Ude-Uke/ Kizami-Zuki/Gyaku-Zuki/Gedan-Barai	*Kōkutsu-Dachi Zenkutsu-Dachi Zenkutsu-Dachi*	5	Stepping forward and backwards
Shutō-Uke/ Mae-Kizami-Geri/Nukite	*Kōkutsu-Dachi Zenkutsu-Dachi*	5	Stepping forward and backwards
Mae-Geri/Mawashi-Geri/Jōdan-Uraken-Uchi/Chūdan-Gyaku-Zuki/Gedan-Barai	*Zenkutsu-Dachi*	3	Turn, same back
Mae-Geri/Yoko-Geri Kekomi/Jōdan-Shutō-Uchi/Chūdan-Gyaku-Zuki/Gedan-Barai	*Zenkutsu-Dachi*	3	Turn, same back
Yoko-Geri-Keage/ Chūdan-Gyaku-Zuki/ Gedan-Barai	*Kiba-Dachi Zenkutsu-Dachi Kiba-Dachi*	3	Turn, same back
Ushiro-Geri	*Zenkutsu-Dachi*	3	Turn, same back

Facing the front in *Zenkutsu Dachi*, kick *Mae-Geri* forward, *Yoko-Geri-Kekomi* to the side and *Mawashi-Geri* forward with the same leg. Repeat from opposite stance with other back leg.

Brown Belt - 1st Kyu

With 2 red stripes

Technique	Stance	No.	Additional informatic
Kihon (**Basics**)			
Sanbon-Zuki	*Zenkutsu-Dachi*	5	Stepping forward, turn *Mae-Geri/Sanbon-Zuki*
Age-Uke/Mae-Geri/ Gyaku-Zuki/Gedan Barai	*Zenkutsu-Dachi*	5	Stepping forward and backwards
Soto-Ude-Uke/ Yoko-Empi-Uchi/ Jōdan-Uraken-Uchi/ Chūdan-Gyaku-Zuki/ Gedan-Barai	*Zenkutsu-Dachi Kiba-Dachi Kiba-Dachi Zenkutsu-Dachi Zenkutsu-Dachi*	5	Stepping forward and backwards
Uchi-Ude-Uke/ Kizami-Zuki/Gyaku-Zuki/Gedan-Barai	*Kōkutsu-Dachi Zenkutsu-Dachi Zenkutsu-Dachi*	5	Stepping forward and Backwards
Shutō-Uke/ Mawashi-Kizami-Geri/ Nukite	*Kōkutsu-Dachi Zenkutsu-Dachi*	5	Stepping forward and backwards
Mae-Geri/Mawashi Geri/ Jōdan-Uraken-Uchi/ Chūdan-Gyaku-Zuki/ Gedan-Barai	*Zenkutsu-Dachi*	3	Turn, same back
Mae-Geri/Yoko-Geri Kekomi/Jōdan-Shutō-Uchi Chūdan-Gyaku-Zuki/ Gedan-Barai	*Zenkutsu-Dachi*	3	Turn, same back
Yoko-Geri-Keage/ Chūdan-Gyaku-Zuki/ Gedan-Barai	*Kiba-Dachi Zenkutsu-Dachi Kiba-Dachi*	3	Turn, same back
Ushiro-Geri/ Gyaku-Zuki	*Zenkutsu-Dachi*	3	Turn, same back

Brown Belt - 1st Kyu
Continued

Technique	Stance	No.	Additional information
Yoko-Geri-Kekomi (front leg)/Mae-Geri (back leg)	Stepping forward in Zenkutsu-Dachi	3	Turn, same back
Mae-Geri/Yoko-Geri-Kekomi	Zenkutsu-Dachi	3	Turn, same back
Mae-Geri/Mawashi-Geri	Zenkutsu-Dachi	3	Turn, same back
Mae-Geri/Yoko-Geri-Kekomi/Ushiro-Geri	Facing the front in Zenkutsu-Dachi. Repeat on opposite side	3	Performing consecutive kicks on the same leg
Kumite (Sparring)	Kihon-Ippon-Kumite (1-attack-sparring)		Sets 1-5 right attack only
	Jiyū-Ippon-Kumite (Semi-free-1-attack-sparring)		Set 3 attack from both sides
Kata (Formal exercise)	A choice of one of the following:		Kanku-Dai, Enpi, Jion, Jitte, Ji'in Plus any previous Kata

Black Belt
Shodan: 1st Degree

Technique	Stance	No.	Additional informatic
Kihon (Basics)			
Kizami-Zuki/Mae-Geri/ Sanbon-Zuki	*Zenkutsu-Dachi*	3	Stepping forward, turn same back
Age-Uke/Mae-Geri/ Gyaku-Zuki/Gedan-Barai	*Zenkutsu-Dachi*	3	Stepping forward and backwards
Soto-Ude-Uke/ Yoko-Empi-Uchi/ Jōdan-Uraken-Uchi/ Chūdan-Gyaku-Zuki/ Gedan-Barai	*Zenkutsu-Dachi Kiba-Dachi Kiba-Dachi Zenkutsu-Dachi Zenkutsu-Dachi*	3	Stepping forward and backwards
Uchi-Ude-Uke/ Kizami-Zuki/Gyaku-Zuki/ Gedan-Barai	*Kōkutsu-Dachi Zenkutsu-Dachi Zenkutsu-Dachi*	3	Stepping forward and backwards
Shutō-Uke/ Mawashi-Kizami-Geri/ Nukite	*Kōkutsu-Dachi Zenkutsu-Dachi*	3	Stepping forward and backwards
Mae-Geri/Mawashi-Geri/ Jōdan-Uraken-Uchi/ Chūdan-Gyaku-Zuki/ Gedan-Barai	*Zenkutsu-Dachi*	3	Turn, same back
Mae-Geri/Yoko-Geri Kekomi/Jōdan-Shutō-Uchi/ Chūdan-Gyaku-Zuki/ Gedan-Barai	*Zenkutsu-Dachi*	3	Turn, same back
Yoko-Geri-Keage/ Chūdan-Gyaku-Zuki/ Gedan-Barai	*Kiba-Dachi Zenkutsu-Dachi Kiba-Dachi*	3	Turn, same back

N.B. All *Kihon* and combination techniques are performed from *Jiyū-Dachi* (Free-fighting stance)

Black Belt Shodan: 1st Degree – Continued

Technique	Stance	No.	Additional information
Kihon (Basics)			
Gyaku-Zuki/Mae-Geri/ Mawashi-Geri turn Shutō-Uke/ Gyaku-Zuki	*Zenkutsu-Dachi*	3	Turn, same back
Step back *Age-Uke*, step forward *Mawashi-Geri* (back leg), *Jōdan Uraken-uchi/Chūdan Oi-Zuki*	*Zenkutsu-Dachi*	3	Turn, same back
Mawashi-Kizami-Geri/ Ushiro-Geri/Jōdan-Ura-ken-Uchi/Chūdan-Gyaku Zuki	*Zenkutsu-Dachi*	3	Turn, same back
Kizami-Yoko-Geri-Kekomi, step forward *Mae-Geri/Oi-Zuki/ GyakuZuki*	*Zenkutsu-Dachi*	3	Turn, same back
Yoko-Geri-Keage/Yoko Geri-Kekomi with the same leg	*Kiba-Dachi*	3	Turn, same back
Mae-Geri/Yoko-Geri-Kekomi/Mawashi-Geri/Ushiro-Geri	Facing the front in *Zenkutsu-Dachi*. Repeat on opposite side.	3	Performing 4 consecutive kicks with the same leg.

Kumite (Sparring)

Kihon-Ippon-Kumite, Sets 1-5, attacking both sides.
Jiyū-Ippon-Kumite, Sets 1-5, attacking both sides.
Jiyū-Kumite against 2 Dan-grades, fighting consecutively.

Kata (Formal exercise)

A choice of one of the following: *Kanku-Dai, Enpi, Jion, Jitte, Ji'in, Gankaku* or *Hangetsu*, plus a previous Kata of the examiner's choice.

Oral Examination (To assess the student's character, thinking and maturity.)

1-10 in *Japanese*

'I'll Never remember that!'
'Oh yes you will - here's how!'
Just memorise this short story:
Mr. *Itchi-Knee* (1+2) and his friend Mr. *San-She* (3+4) loved dancing. Every night they would *Go* (5) and *Rock* (6) the night away with their girl-friends *Shichi* (7) and *Hachi* (8) to the funky music of the *Ku-Ju* (9+10) band.

1 Ichi	2 Ni
3 San	4 She
5 Go	6 Rokku
7 Shichi	8 Hachi
9 Ku	10 Ju

Martin's Muscles

HELP!

...and they have

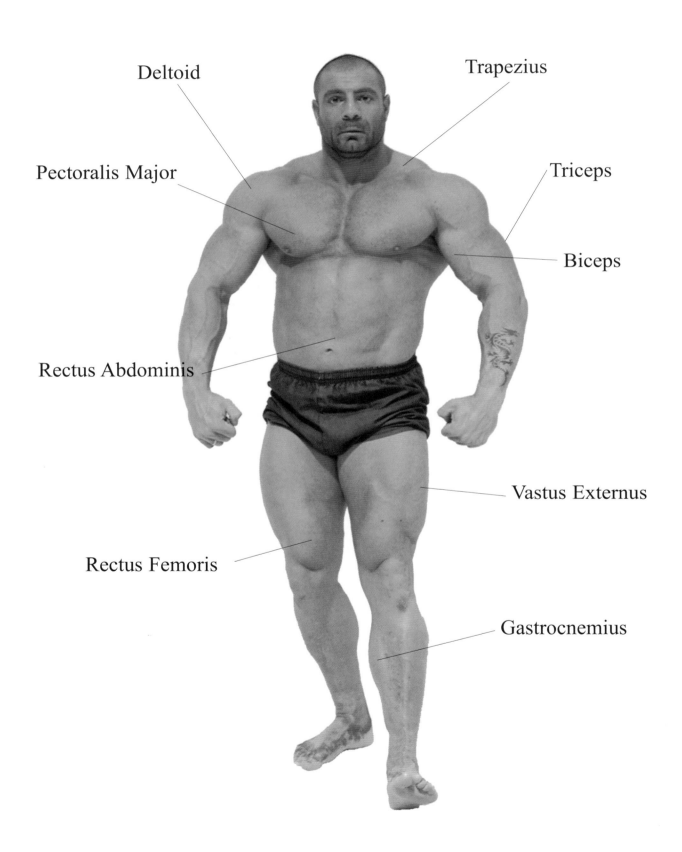

Deltoid

Trapezius

Pectoralis Major

Triceps

Biceps

Rectus Abdominis

Vastus Externus

Rectus Femoris

Gastrocnemius

Latin names!

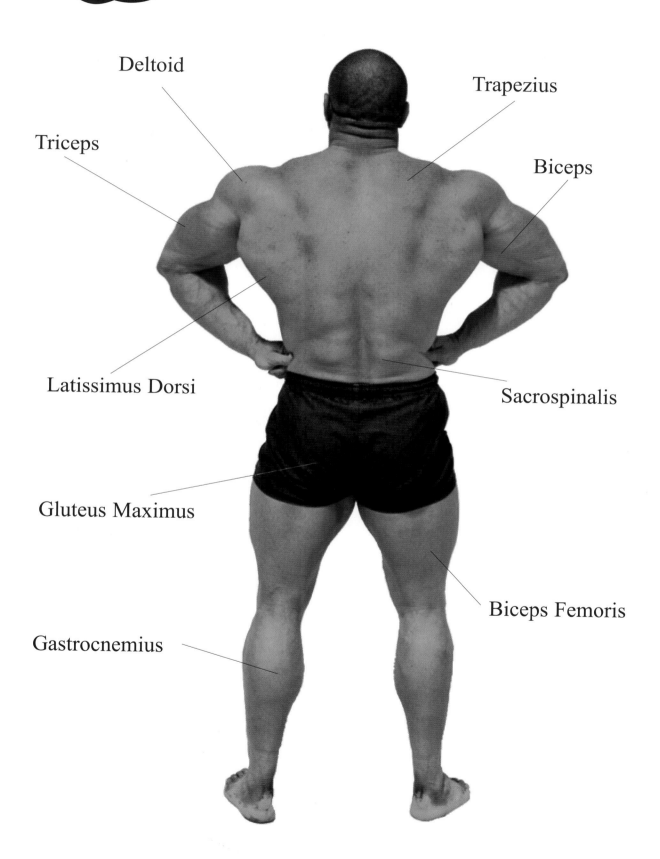

Deltoid

Trapezius

Triceps

Biceps

Latissimus Dorsi

Sacrospinalis

Gluteus Maximus

Biceps Femoris

Gastrocnemius

Muscles Quiz Time

1

2

3

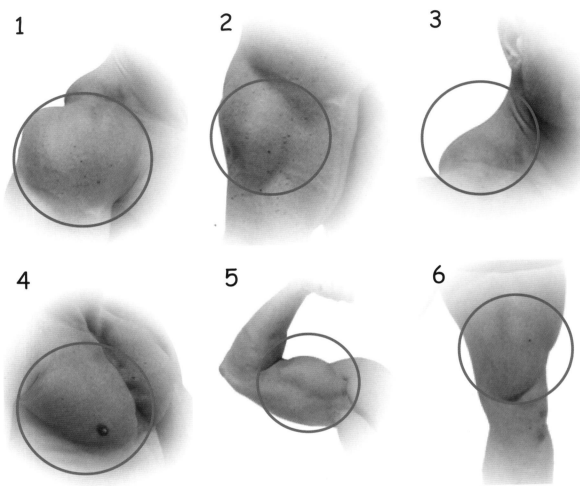

4

5

6

answers here

7

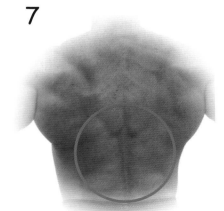

1..
2..
3..
4..
5..
6..
7..

Tournaments and Competitions

Just how important are they?

The fact that the Father of modern day *Karate, Gichin Funakoshi*, was totally against them says a lot. He saw his beloved art, which he had given his life to, heading on a downward spiral with the arrival of *Karate* matches and contests.

His fear was that the martial art, the *budō* spirit, along with it's associated disciplines and philosophy would be replaced by nothing more than a glorified sport.

However, with hindsight, it does appear the great man's fears were largely unjustified. Personally, I think the fact that traditional *Karate* is far bigger now than it ever was, is mainly due to *Funakoshi's* extraordinary contribution to *Karate-dō*.

The on-set of sport *Karate* soon after the Master's death in 1957 was inevitable. Had he lived he could not have stopped it.

Fifty years on, things are quite different.

Karate tournaments are held all over the world and provide much enjoyment to many.

However, to the traditionalist, the importance competitions assume is often no more than 10% of his training time; but it has to be acknowledged, there are numerous benefits to be gained.

It allows contestants to pit their skills against each other in a way that is the closest they can come to real combat. *Jiyū-Kumite* (free-sparring) develops confidence and improves timing and distancing. Whilst encouraging success, it also teaches participants to deal with failure, should it come.

In life, there may be winners and losers, and it may not be possible to be in the former category all the time, but regardless, we are all participants. It was *Funakoshi* who reminded us that 'winning or losing took second place to participation.'

Of vital importance is the ability of a winning contestant to exhibit humility. Behaving with respect and decorum whilst naturally being filled with elation, is essential.

These aspects were obviously of great concern to *Gichin Funakoshi* all those years ago.

Today thousands of people enjoy *Karate* tournaments all over the world and their popularity justifies the path that *Karate* has taken, to an extent that it is virtually essential that all *Kyu* grades should have 'some' experience in *dōjō* or tournament freestyle. Reaching black-belt level without it, would reveal a serious weakness in the student's competence.

However - bear in mind, it's no more than 10% of overall *Karate* training - so let's keep things in perspective.

Remember

Always do your best. Only 100% effort is acceptable. This applies at school during lessons and elsewhere, no matter what you are doing.

Always respect your parents, teachers, classmates and above all, yourself.

Always refrain from using bad language - let it have no place in your life. It's vulgar and lazy. Instead find a way to express yourself in the Queen's English.

Always be of good behaviour; there's no reason to be otherwise. Demonstrate politeness wherever you go.

Always help wherever possible. A small gesture by you may mean a huge amount to someone else.

Be the best you can be -
why not?

Now here's an interesting fact. Most people during their lives use only 10% of their mental capabilities. Now I hear you ask, 'what happens to the other 90%?'
Well in most cases - it remains dormant.
Let's consider the human brain for just a moment.

It really is the world's most powerful yet versatile computer. Within its confines, it boasts six trillion cells, and amazingly, each cell has half-a-million communication devises. When you have a thought, it's hard to imagine it travels around your brain at two hundred miles an hour - but it does!

So to be the best you can be, you need to harness as much of the brain's capabilities as possible.

Looking at the body's physical side for just a moment, the more you use it, the better shape it will be in. The old adage 'use it or lose it', makes a lot of sense.   Some interesting information has come to light in recent years concerning brain cells. Let's take the case of a bank manager for example - he's perfect, although it's all imagined.

He usually joins banking as a junior and gradually works his way up the ladder till he is promoted to branch manager. With time he may go on to larger branches and increased responsibility.

By middle age he is considered successful, and shoulders his many responsibilities well. His salary is ample, enabling him to satisfy most of his desires he has for himself and his family. At the office he works hard, dealing with people from all walks of life - from high powered business men, to students opening their first bank account.

Throughout his long career, he maintains one eye permanently fixed on an early retirement at sixty, and a welcome escape from the daily rat-race.

When that time finally arrives, he collects the customary gold watch, has his hand shaken by all and sundry, and leaves the office to enjoy his long awaited retirement. He moves away to the seaside, Eastbourne, or some other such Shangri-la, buys his own deck-chair - and flops.

It doesn't take long for his brain to realise it's not wanted anymore - so it starts to shut down.

Within a week - **he's dead!**

Recent scientific research has proved we need to rethink this scenario and perhaps undergo a little brain re-programming. As we grow older brain cells die, so working hard during the early part of your life while you are physically and mentally capable, before relaxing and being 'put out to grass', seemed to be most sensible.

Now, scientists have thrown this theory into disarray by proving older people can quite easily grow new brain cells. Don't retire just because you are sixty-five. Take up a new career, go back to college or university, start a new job, write a book, travel, but whatever you do, keep your brain active and *keep those cells multiplying!*

This book's most important message

'*K*arate is not about fighting, it is about *not fighting.*

It is primarily defensive - not offensive.

It's true, you could inflict a great deal of damage on a person, however, just because you are able to doesn't mean *you have to*. To a degree, if you have to fight - you've failed.

What I'm really saying here is this:

Nine times out of ten, a fight can be avoided. On most occasions it is possible to talk your way out of it, or avoid certain places or individuals altogether.

Just on the very odd occasion will it be necessary to use your *Karate* skills in order to protect yourself, family or friends. Using them in self-defence is acceptable but avoiding an altercation (argument or fight) is far preferable.

So lets assume that your fighting ability is not required in day to day life, then there has to be other benefits to be gained from *Karate* training that can be utilised on a daily basis - and there are! Vastly improved fitness is one, along with a much better standard of health, well-being and confidence.

Think of it like this - by avoiding a confrontation, you are actually using your *Karate* skills.'

Glossary

Japanese	Pronunciation	English
Age-Uke	Ah-gay-oo-kay	Upper-rising-block
Age-Zuki	Ah-gay-zoo-key	Upper-rising-punch
Bassai-Dai	Bass-ar-ee-dah-ee	To penetrate a fortress
Bō	Boh	A Staff
Budō	Boo-do (o as in orange)	Martial ways
Chinte	Chin-tay	Chinese-hands
Choku-Zuki	Cho-koo-zoo-key	Straight-punch
Chūdan	Choo-dahn	Middle level
Dachi	Dah-chee	Stance
Dan	Dahn	Level (black-belt grade)
Dō	Dough	The way of
Dō-gi	Dough-ghee	*Karate* uniform
Dōjō	Dough-joe	The way place, training hall
Empi	Em-pee	Flying-swallow
Empi	Em-pee	Elbow
Empi-Uchi	Em-pee-oo-chee	Elbow-strike
Empi-Uke	Em-pee-oo-kay	Elbow-block
Fumikomi	Foo-me-koh-me	Stamping-kick
Fudo-Dachi	Foo-dough-dah-chee	Immovable-stance
Gankaku	Gahn-car-koo	Crane-on-a-rock
Gedan	Geh-dahn	Lower level
Gedan-Barai	Geh-dahn-baa-rye	Lower-parry
Gedan-Zuki	Geh-dahn-zoo-key	Lower-punch
Geri (Keri)	Geh-rhee	Kick
Gi	Ghee	Practice suit
Gohon-kumite	Go-hon-koo-me-tay	Five-step-sparring
Gyaku	Gya-koo	Reverse
Gyaku-Zuki	Gya-koo-zoo-key	Reverse-punch

Japanese	Pronunciation	English
Hachiji-Dachi	Hah-chee-gee-dah-chee	Natural open-leg-stance
Haishu-Uchi	Hi-shoe-oo-chee	Back-hand-strike
Haishu-Uke	Hi-shoe-oo-kay	Back-hand-block
Haitō	Hi-toe	Ridge-hand
Haitō-Uchi	Hi-toe-oo-chee	Ridge-hand-strike
Haitō-Uke	Hi-toe-oo-kay	Ridge-hand-block
Haiwan	Hi-wharn	Back-arm
Haiwan-Uke	Hi-whan-oo-kay	Back-arm-block
Hangetsu	Hahn-get-sue	Half-moon
Hanmi	Hahn-me	Half-facing-position
Hara	Hah-rah	Concept of spiritual centre
Hara-kiri	Hah-rah-key-ree	Literally: Belly cut
Heian	Hey-un	Peaceful mind
Heian Shodan	Hey-un-sho-dahn	Peaceful mind 1st level
Heian Nidan	Hey-un-knee-dahn	Peaceful mind 2nd level
Heian Sandan	Hey-un-san-dahn	Peaceful mind 3rd level
Heian Yondan	Hey-un-yon-dahn	Peaceful mind 4th level
Heian Godan	Hey-un-go-dahn	Peaceful mind 5th level
Heisoku-Dachi	Hey-sock-oo-dah-chee	Informal attention stance
Hidari	He-dar-rhee	Left
Hiraken	He-rah-ken	Fore-knuckle fist
Hiza	He-zar	Knee
Hiza-Geri	He-zar-geh-rhee	Knee-kick
Honbu	Hon-boo	Main training hall
Ippon-Ken	Eepon-ken	One-knuckle-fist
Ippon-Nukite	Eepon-noo-key-tay	One-finger-spear-hand
Ji'in	Gee-inn	Named after temple, Jion
Jion	Gee-on	Temple
Jitte	Gee-tay	Ten-hands
Jiyū-Ippon	Gee-you-eepon	Semi-free-one-attack
Jiyū-Kumite	Gee-you-koo-me-tay	Free-sparring
Jōdan	Joe-dahn	Upper level

Japanese	Pronunciation	English
Jūji-Uke	Jew-gee-oo-kay	X-block
Ka	Car	Person/student
Kage-Uke	Kah-gay-oo-kay	Hooking-block
Kage-Zuki	Kah-gay-zoo-key	Hooking-punch
Kakatō	Kah-kar-toe	Heel
Kake-Uke	Kah-keh-oo-kay	Hooking-block
Kakiwake-Uke	Kah-key-wah-kay-ookay	Wedge-block
Kamikaze	Kah-me-kah-zay	Divine wind. Suicide pilots
Kanku-Dai	Kahn-koo-dah-ee	To look at the sky
Kara	Kah-rah	Empty-Chinese
Kata	Kah-tah	Formal exercise
Keage	Key-ah-gay	Snap
Keitō-Uke	Kay-toe-oo-kay	Chicken-head-wrist-block
Kekomi	Kay-koh-me	Thrust
Keri	Keh-rhee	Kick
Ki	Key	Inner power (Spirit)
Kiai	Key eye	Shout to unite Ki & physical
Kiba-Dachi	Key-bah-dah-chee	Straddle-leg-stance
Kihon Ippon	Key-on-eepon	Basic-one-attack
Kime	Key-may	Focus
Kizami-Zuki	Key-za-mee zoo-key	Front-snap-punch
Kin-Geri	Kin-geh-rhee	Groin-kick
Kōkutsu-Dachi	Ko-koot-sue-dah-chee	Back-stance
Koshi	Ko-shi	Ball-of-foot
Kumade	Koo-mar-day	Bear-hand
Kumite	Koo-me-tay	Sparring
Kun	U as in ou in could	Oath
Kyu	Quew	Rank below black-belt
Ma-ai	Mah-ee	Distancing
Mae	Mah-eh	Front
Mae-Geri	Mah-eh-geh-rhee	Front-kick
Makiwara	Mar-key-wa-rah	Striking-post

Japanese	Pronunciation	English
Mawashi-Geri	Ma-wa-she-ge-rhee	Roundhouse-kick
Mawashi-Zuki	Ma-wa-she-zoo-key	Roundhouse-punch
Mawate	Mah-wa-tay	Turn
Migi	Me-ghee	Right
Mikazuki-Geri	Me-car-zoo-key-geree	Crescent-kick
Mizu-No-Kokoro	Me-zoo-no-ko-ko-roe	Mind-like-water
Mokuso	Moku- sow (crops)	Meditation
Morote-Uke	Mo-ro-tay-oo-kay	Augmented-forearm-block
Morote-Zuki	Mo-ro-tay-zoo-kay	Augmented-block
Musubi-Dachi	Moo-soo-bee-dahchee	Attention-stance
Nagashi-Uke	Nah-gah-she-oo-kay	Sweeping-block
Naha-Te	Nah-ha-tay	Okinawan *Karate* School
Nakadaka-Ippon-Ken	Nar-ka-dah-car-eepon-ken	One-knuckle-fist
Nami-Ashi	Nar-me-ar-she	Inside leg block
Neko-Ashi-Dachi	Neh-ko-ar-she-dar-chi	Cat-stance
Nidan-Geri	Nee-dahn-ge-rhee	Two level kick
Nihon Nukite	Kneehon-Noo-key-tay	Two finger Spear-hand
Nukite	Noo-key-tay	Spear-hand-thrust
Obi	Oh-bee	Belt/sash
Oi-Zuki	Oi-zoo-key	Stepping-punch
Okinawa-Te	Oh-kin-ar-wa-tay	Okinawan *Karate* school
Rei	Ray	Bow
Ren-Zuki	Wren-zoo-key	Alternate punching
Ryu	Ree-you	School (style) of *Karate*
Sanbon-Kumite	San-Bonn-koo-me-tay	Three-step sparring
Seiken	Say-ken	Fore-fist
Seiza	Say-zar	Japanese kneeling position
Sempai	Sem-pie	Senior
Sensei	Sen-say	Teacher
Seppuku	Sep-poo-koo	Ritual suicide

Japanese	Pronunciation	English
Shihan	She-harn	Master, 6th Dan and above
Shiro	She-roe	White
Shizentai	She-zen-tah-ee	Natural-stance
Shutō	Shoe-toe	Knife-hand
Shutō-Uchi	Shoe-toe-oo-chee	Knife-hand-strike
Shutō-Uke	Shoe-toe-oo-kay	Knife-hand-block
Sochin	Saw-chin	A formal exercise
Sokutō	Sow-koo-toe	Foot-edge
Soto-Ude-Uke	So-toh-oo-day-oo-kay	Outside-forearm-block
Taikyoku	Tar-eek-yo-koo	First Cause
Taikyoku-Shodan	Tykeyo-koo sho-dahn	Formal exercise
Tai-Sabaki	Tye-sar-bar-key	Body shifting
TASK		Traditional *Shōtōkan* Ass.
Tate-Shutō-Uke	Tar-tay-shootoe-ooka	Vertical Knife-hand-block
Te	Tay	Hand
Teishō	Tay-show	Palm-heel
Teishō-Uchi	Tay-show-oo-chee	Palm-heel-strike
Teishō-Uke	Tay-show-oo-key	Palm-heel-block
Tekki-Nidan	Tey-key-knee-dahn	2nd level formal exercise
Tekki-Sandan	Tey-key-sahn-dahn	3rd level formal exercise
Tekki-Shodan	Tey-key-show-dahn	1st level formal exercise
Tettsui	Tet-sooie	Bottom-fist
Tettsui-Uchi	Tet-sooie oo-chee	Bottom-fist-strike
Tobi	Toe-be	Jump
Tsuki	Tsue-key	Punch
Uchi	Oo-chee	Strike
Uchi-Ude-Uke	Oo-chee-oo-kay	Inside-forearm-block
Ude	Oo-day	Forearm
Uke	Oo-kay	Block
Unsu	Oon-sue	Hands of the cloud
Ura-Zuki	Oo-rah-zoo-key	Close-punch
Uraken	Oo-rah-ken	Backfist

Japanese	Pronunciation	English
Ushiro-Enpi *Ushiro-Geri* *Ushiro-Mawashi-Geri*	Oo-she-row-em-pee Oo-she-row-geh-rhee Oo-she-row-mah-wah-she- geh-rhee	Reverse-elbow Back-kick Back-roundhouse-kick
Washide *Wankan*	Wah-she-day Wahn-kahn	Eagle-hand (beak) Shortest *Shōtōkan Kata*
Yama-Zuki *Yame* *Yoi* *Yoko* *Yoko-Empi-Uchi* *Yoko-Geri*	Yah-mah-zoo-key Yar-may As in boy Yoh-koh Yo-ko empee-oo-chee Yo-ko-geh-rhee	U-Punch Stop-finish Ready Side Side-elbow-strike Side-kick
Zazen *Zen* *Zenkutsu-Dachi* *Zuki*	Zar-zen Zen Zen-koo-tsue-dah-chee Zoo-key	Seated-meditation A form of Buddhism Forward-stance (front) Punch

Recommended Reading

Title: | **The Begineers Guide to Shōtōkan Karate**
Author & Publisher: | John van Weenen
Distributors: | Vine House Distribution Ltd.
Tel. 01825 723398
Blitz Corp Ltd.
Tel. 0208 3178280
Paperback: ISBN 0-9517660-4-X
RRP £14.95 in UK
Pages: 532

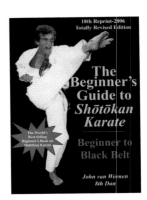

Title: | **Advanced Shōtōkan Karate Kata**
Author & Publisher: | John van Weenen
Distributors: | Vine House Distribution Ltd.
Tel: 01825 723398
Blitz Corp. Ltd.
Tel. 0208 3178280
Paperback: ISBN 0-9517660-1-5
RRP £12.95 in UK
Pages: 196

Title: | **In Funakoshi's Footsteps**
Author & Publisher: | John van Weenen
Distributors: | Vine House Distribution Ltd.
Tel: 01825 723398
Blitz Corp. Ltd.
Tel. 0208 3178280
Paperback: ISBN 0-9517660-9-0
RRP £9.95 in UK Pages: 530
Hardback: ISBN 0-9517660-5-8
RRP £14.95 in UK
Pages 530

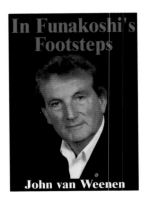

Title: **Injury Free Karate**
Author :   Paul Perry
Publisher & Distributor: A. C. Black
                Blitz Corp. Ltd.
                Tel: 0208 3178280
                ISBN 0 7136 3573 8

Title: **Shōtōkan Karate International
                Kata**
                Volumes 1 & 2
Author: Hirokazu Kanazawa
Publisher & Distributor: Shōtōkan Karate International
                Mona Books UK www.monabooks.co.uk
                ISBN - None recorded

Title: **Moving Zen**
Author: C. W. Nicol
Publisher & Distributor: William Morrow & Co. Inc.
                New York
                Blitz Corp. Ltd.
                ISBN 0-688-02871-3

Title: **Karate-Dō Kyohan**
Author: Gichin Funakoshi
Publisher & Distributor: Kodansha International
                Blitz Corp. Ltd.
                ISBN 0-7063-1996-6

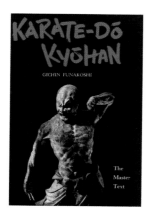

Title: **Karate-Dō-My Way of Life**
Author: Gichin Funakoshi
Publisher & Distributor: Kodansha International
Blitz Corp. Ltd.
ISBN 0-87011-463-8

Title: **The Twenty Guiding Principles of Karate**
Author: Gichin Funakoshi
Publisher & Distributor: Kodansha International
Mona Books UK
www.monabooks.co.uk
ISBN 4-7700-2796-6

Other books by the same author

Title:
Author & Publisher:
Distributor

Task Force Albania - An Odyssey
John van Weenen
Vine House Distribution Ltd.
Tel. 01825 723398
Paperback:
ISBN 0-951-7660-8-2
RRP UK £9.95
Pages: 290

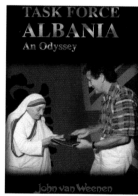

Title:

Author & Publisher:
Distributor:

TASK Force Albania - The Kosovo Connection
John van Weenen
Vine House Distribution Ltd.
Tel. 01825 723398
Paperback: ISBN 0-951-7660-3-1
RRP UK £9.95
Pages: 236

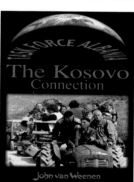

Coming Soon

Karate for Children Volume II - Kata

Karate for Children Volume III - Kumite

Notes

Notes